Processing the Law
A Holistic Approach

Preliminary Edition

Frank Primiani, J.D.

Green River Community College

Cover and interior illustrations by Brian Rabold.

www.kendallhunt.com
Send all inquiries to:
4050 Westmark Drive
Dubuque, IA 52004-1840

Copyright © 2009 by Kendall Hunt Publishing Company

ISBN 978-0-7575-6617-2

Printed in the United States of America
10 9 8 7 6 5 4 3 2 1

Contents

Introduction: Course Design and Key Descriptors

As we proceed through this class, I will often give a one or two word summary for each chapter we are studying. Having just one or two words in mind will help create a core idea of what everything in the chapter is about. In this way, I hope that students will see the connection between the word descriptors and ideas discussed each chapter.

I would like to do the same thing for the class as a whole, but since we are talking about a greater mass of information, there are several descriptors that can be used to better conceptualize the overall design of these law classes. Keep these descriptors in mind if you ever find yourself wondering why we are doing this or that activity in class. Usually, it will be part of the design or philosophical underpinnings for the class. Here are the key class concepts you should remember when the "Why?" Question comes to mind:

1. Holistic: A holistic perspective attempts to view each student as a complete human being. That is, not just a brain sitting in a chair, but a brain that is connected to emotions and actions as well. Thus, a holistic class is designed to engage each student's cognitive or thinking self, his/her affective or emotional self, and each student's action oriented, or doing self. As Psychologists might tell us, these 3 interrelated parts of the self are usually in a congruent state. For example, if a person is thinking depressive thoughts, they are probably also having depressed feelings, and acting in a depressed manner. The mind influences the emotions, which can influence behaviors and vice versa. Some class activities are designed primarily to stimulate intellectual thinking, such as traditional exams, assignments, and papers. Some class activities are designed mostly to engage emotional responses, such as resolving issues or conflict that may arise in a group work situation. Still other tasks will require a coordinated action plan to put together a collaborative work product or case method presentation. In these ways, it is hoped that each student will have a total emersive experience in learning not only how the law functions in a society, but also what it feels like to resolve a conflict or dispute in a work setting, and in actively creating a work product which transmits such knowledge to the class as a whole.

HOLISTIC

2. Case Method: The case method approach studies the subject matter through the analysis of real world situations. In this class, these will be in the form of real legal cases that have been heard and resolved in the Federal or State legal systems. Working in groups, students will prepare and present their individual portion of a group effort in presenting the essential and relevant details of each case, and its relationship to the textbook concepts and to life in general. The work group will analyze each case from the perspective of the court that decided it, and transmit that understanding to the class in a power point format. Analysis means to take apart. Using a theoretical model for analysis, each group with break down the case into its component parts, learn to assess each part, and re-synthesis the parts into a coherent and interesting whole, the final work product. This activity is not fundamentally different from many analytic activities we engage in other contexts. For example, an auto mechanic might take apart a carburetor into its parts, assess each functional part perhaps fixing or replacing some, and then put the carburetor back together in an improved condition. This sort of analysis and synthetic process is fairly easy to understand in the tangible world, but it also happens in the intangible world of ideas and complex thought. Each legal case is constructed of such complex facts or ideas, and it will be the charge of each group to perform such intellectual dissection, and present your findings to the class.

Okay you bees, tell me the relevant details for gathering nectar...

CASE METHOD

3. Transparency: The notion of transparency is a concept that allows each student to clearly see and understand the standards that will be used to assess student performance in the class. In this fashion, the student should not have to guess at how or why a particular grade was given for an assignment. Because the grading standards are known to all before the assignment is given, and those same standards are used to grade the assignment, each student can prepare their work in anticipation that such standards will be used. This will thereby allow each student or group to self assess their own work, prior to its presentation.

TRANSPARENCY

4. Hive Mind: The metaphor of the hive mind is used to convey a notion that any group of individuals striving to meet similar goals can be viewed a part of a greater whole. Each separate member of the group or "hive" has the ability to benefit each other member of the hive. That is, information and knowledge is dispersed throughout the group. At any given time, any member of the group can have access to information, knowledge, or concepts that can be applied to a particular problem that may indirectly benefit the whole group. Viewed in this way, key information can come from any member of the group, as each member of the group may have specialized experience, knowledge, or talents unavailable to other group members. Stated in a more simplified form, it is the notion that "we is smarter than me". Information and knowledge is not unidirectional, but multidirectional. Solutions to problems can emerge from any group member, or can be constructed piecemeal by successive contributions from various members. No longer is the professor or class instructor viewed as the dispenser of all knowledge, but largely as a facilitator or "hive manager" that helps to organize a structure for group interaction.

5. Question Driven: The intellectual energy fueling the attainment of knowledge are the questions the mind generates in considering matters of concern. In other words, knowledge is not driven by answers, but by questions. Even after a particular answer is reached, there is always another question that can be asked about the outcome. The active mind is viewed as a question generator, while the passive mind either has no desire to ask questions, or is not thinking well enough to produce any questions. In this class, I use the frequency of questions as somewhat of a barometer for determining the active intellectual state of the class. When the frequency of questions declines, I find that a class quiz can often refocus and sharpen the class consciousness about questions.

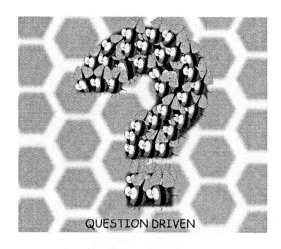

QUESTION DRIVEN

6. Active learning: The active engagement of the learner in relevant activities is often a good way to learn new concepts and skills. This is especially true when a class contains much abstract content, such as the case with law. Learning by doing is often a good approach to not only keep the student stimulated in the subject matter, but also counteract any tendencies for passive apathy. When students are asked to perform, they often rise to the occasion because they generally want to display their talents in a larger context, and be viewed as competent contributors to the class effort. For some, there is also the deterrent effect of avoiding any humiliation that might come from appearing to be unprepared or not understanding the material. It is possible that there may be an affective or emotional cost to the student who may not fair well in a particular activity but, in my experience, a student's self perception of poor performance generally results in an increased motivation to do better in the future. In other words, a student's innate self efficacy often counters possible negative effects of a less than desirable performance.

7. Skill development: Good thinking is an acquired skill, much like any other skill we might learn as human beings. As in the case of a gifted musician or athlete, continued practice makes the difference between an amateur and a professional. This is not to dismiss any genetic tendency of some people to have an inherent advantage at some tasks, but all else being equal, it is often the practice that makes the difference. Think of the brain as a muscle that must be used to stay in good shape. In fact, recent scientific evidence clearly establishes the importance of keeping the mind active and engaged in order to avoid senescence and dementia. Other studies on lab rats showed that animals that were given lots of "rat toys" to keep their brains stimulated not only did better on rat intelligence tests, but actually grew more grey matter in their brains. Not long ago such increase in brain grey matter would have been thought unattainable! In keeping with this idea of skill development, it is useful to think of the classroom as a "mental gym", where students can come to work out their brains and minds (there is a subtle difference). No one would think of going to a weight room or traditional gym to stand around and watch others work out, while wondering why they don't have "6-pack abs". You can't get stronger by

watching, but must develop your skills by doing! In short, don't forget to wear your "mental sweatpants" before coming to class.

8. Process Orientation: The world is constructed of both substance and process. The substance is the "stuff" or content of life, while the process includes the procedures, directions, or actions involved in creating or making the stuff. For example, think of that traditional Thanksgiving dinner, with the turkey as the main course. Suppose a person wanted to cook such a dinner, but had never cooked a turkey before. They buy the best grade turkey they can find and decide to cook it at 900 degrees for 45 minutes (no, not in the deep fryer!). They would have something very raw on the inside and very burnt on the outside. Despite having good substance (the bird), their process or procedure left something to be desired. On the other hand, a person could have an excellent recipe for grandma's turkey with Oyster-cornbread stuffing, and all the trimmings and follow the recipe to a tee, only to discover that the turkey had been left out too long and got salmonella! In this latter case, the process was excellent but the substance went bad. Neither of these situations will produce a very good meal. It is the combination of a good substance and a good process that leads to a palatable outcome. Not only is this dichotomy true in the tangible world of turkeys, but also in the intangible world of law. The substance of law are the laws as they are they are made. That is, the Statutes, Regulations, Ordinances, precedent case law, or Constitutions. The process or procedure of law is the application or enforcement of the laws. The famous quote of Bismarck may apply here: "Those that love sausage and respect the law, should watch neither being made". The inference being that sometimes it is a messy and unappealing process. Sometimes, even a little sawdust may get into the sausage, which is a metaphor for corruption that may have a tainting effect on the law. A fair and stable society then necessitates that "good" laws are being made by "good" people, and that "good" procedures are then followed to apply and enforce the laws. Only then can we say that a sense of justice emerges. As we will see later, however, justice can be quite elusive and what seems just today may not be viewed as just tomorrow. Justice is dependent upon the values and culture of society at a given time and place.

In keeping with this substance-process dichotomy, the same notion can be applied to the world of thinking. There is substance or content to our thought, which is the subject we are thinking about, but also the process of thinking through such content. Most college courses are heavily weighted toward conveying the substantive content of a given discipline. That is, the central focus of the course is most often to transmit the content or subject matter to the student in the most efficient manner possible, and then to assess the student's acquisition of such content by various types of examination. In this pedagogical design, the process that the student uses to learn, appreciate, or understand the content is solely the business of the student. Whatever system the student has found to be effective in the past, often by trial and error, is of no concern to the professor as long as the content is mastered on the examination. It is often assumed that the process a student uses to acquire or learn the content is largely irrelevant to the learning. Any old process will do, again, as long as the examinations are passed. This class takes a differing view, which is reflected in the course design. Instead of focusing on the content of the class, we will focus mostly on the process for learning the content. In other words, we aim to process our way through the substantive content. By way of analogy, we focus on building the mental processor and then gradually pour the content in. In my view, the substantive content of the class, in this case law, is inert information. This can function very well as a paper weight, but left to itself, it is useless. Like oil in the ground, it must be extracted, processed, and refined to become useable to the human brain.

What, then, is the recipe or process we shall use to create knowledge and understanding of the substantive content of law? For this we need a model for thinking things through. We can't see, feel, or touch how thinking works. It is abstract. Therefore, we need a conceptual model or theoretical construct to help make this abstract concept more understandable. The Paul-Elder Model of Thinking does just that. It conceptualizes thinking as an interrelationship of constituent parts. Each part performing a specific function that acts in concert with the other parts to form the informal logic of a particular subject matter. As we proceed in this class, we will learn more about what these parts are, how they function, and most importantly how they can be analyzed and assessed. As I state in class, with a process orientation this model for thinking becomes the "key" that will help unlock the content for the course. For those that prefer computer analogies, it will be the "operating system" that underlies the content, much like an Excel spreadsheet must operate within the confines of a Windows operating system. If there are any bugs in the operating system, it will also naturally affect the content of the Excel program. On the other hand, because the operating system can handle and operate a wide array of software programs, it becomes an indispensable, and ubiquitous, part of any computer output. While the output or content of the computer may change or even be forgotten, the features and quality of the underlying operating system must always be working in good order to continue to process in an efficient and effective manner.

9. Continuous quality improvement: In keeping with the nature of skill development addressed above, continued practice and performance of a given task will result in learning improvements over time. Think of any particular skill that you have acquired, and you will easily see the basic reality of this remark. The most common method of quality improvements over time is by trial and error. You fall off a horse, you get back on, fall again, get back on and stay on a little longer until you learn to balance and ride in rhythm with the horse's motion. This is a practical, but often inefficient method for learning improvements. It can be time consuming and, as in the case above, can even

dangerous ....bruises and broken bones take a long time to heal! Perhaps studying horse motions and reading a bit about riding might better prepare the rider for what lies ahead. Even better might be a riding instructor or coach at the side that can give specific feedback during the ride. Thus it is with learning anything, the more we work at it, the better we get. As you proceed in this class, you will also have the advantage of learning from other group presentations. Watch how they present, what techniques or strategies they employ, how well they abide by the standards of good performance. Are they clear, relevant, and accurate? Do they exhibit breath and depth in their presentations? How well do they relate the case to what is discussed in class or what is stated in the textbook? By making an active effort to listen and learn from others, you will also find yourself accelerating your own learning curve. Most importantly, don't hesitate to ask questions of the presenting group, both for their content and also for their process. Staying engaged and focused in this way will reap dividends when it comes time for grades.

CONTINUOUS QUALITY IMPROVEMENT

10. Less Can be More: Most students, including myself, have had the experience of being in a class where a professor was very concerned about "getting through the material" so they could stay on schedule, especially for classes in series. Studies have shown that the coverage of content is too often the primary focus of college courses. Students are often warned that "you are in college now" and that you must make do with the time you have to complete your assigned readings and class assignments. If you need to study late and get less sleep, so be it. Some students are always willing to do what it takes to meet the demands of insistent professors, and there are many more students who would love to have your seat if you are not willing to do what it takes to keep up. Unfortunately, professors are too often oblivious to the fact that each of the students professors may feel the same way! This sort of "pearls to the swine" mentality has permeated those academic ivory towers every bit as much as the ivy has covered it's walls. It has become in some ways, the expected academic ritual that leads to the right of passage. Once established, this ritual becomes part of the historic tradition of what it means to be collegiate. Successful alumni hold their heads high, knowing that they have struggled and survived all of the slings and arrows that this passage requires. There is little or no motivation to

question or challenge this history, because to do so might soften and cheapen the experience for younger students, and devalue the honor of those alumni who have survived the intellectual gristmill.

In this class we have the luxury of not needing to be at any particular place in the content. There is no subsequent law class that students must take for their transfer degree. Where we end up is where we end. We can take time to ask questions and discuss the material, we can consider current events, and the implications of legal cases on our society. We can research legal questions of interest that may come up in the course of those discussions. We can also have some fun along the way. After all, no class needs to be boring. If at any time it seems to be becoming so, someone please snap me out of it!

There is always a scholastic risk associated with allowing for digression along the learning path, and sometimes that divergence may lead to irrelevant or immaterial discussions. On the other hand, sometimes it can also lead to new insights about the subject matter. Every quarter I make it a point to learn something new in the subjects that I am teaching, to see a case from an entirely new perspective, or make reference to a little known footnote in a particular chapter. This keeps the material alive and constantly evolving. Despite covering more or less the same material, no class is ever entirely the same. It is always a new environment under new circumstances, which attains different results. That is partly a consequence of teaching material with no absolute answers, but also has much to do with the interactions of students and the changing perspectives on the material. My role will be not to restrain or inhibit discussion (e.g. students should be seen and not heard), but to channel the discussions in relevant directions. In that manner, the standard of Relevance that I will use to grade your presentations, can also be applied to my direction of class discussions. As we shall see, that is the beauty of objective standards.

In this manner, less coverage of substantive content can often open the door to more in depth understanding of the content that we do cover. Keep this principle in mind as you work on your group presentations… Less can be more, and often is.

11. "We don't plan, we Improvise": This, I am told, is one of the motto's of the Marine Corp. It is a Variation of the adage: "best laid plans often go astray". Despite meticulous planning and preparation, things don't always go as we anticipate. In this class, we try to expect the unexpected, by having contingency plans as backup. This is highly recommended as far as group presentations go. Having a backup of your presentation will allow you to seamlessly flow from your original plan to the contingency plan. You may even get so good at this, that people won't even notice. Hint: I do it all the time. The ability to change plans or strategies on the spur of the moment, not only helps defuse and take stress out of an awkward situation, but can also be a creatively challenging experience that will help you grow in confidence. Being able to adapt and improvise is an important life skill, so I hope you will view it as such, and take advantage of the opportunity to display your prowess at adaptation.

"WE DON'T PLAN, WE IMPROVISE"

12. What Employers Want:
    Years of surveys and studies of employer expectations allow us to better define what kind of generic characteristics employers see as being valuable in their employees. Despite the nature of employment, despite geographic location, and despite organizational structure, most employers are seeing value in the same sorts of characteristics. Hansen and Hansen, Ph.D., "What Employers really want". www.quintcareers.com.

    The typical list ranges from good communication skills (oral and written), excellent thinking and problem solving, good team members, dependable, responsible, and all around nice person (both in and out of the office). While some of these traits may be innate in some, they certainly can also be cultivated and improved through the right kind of practice. You will note that the activities we do in the classroom correlate very well in this listing, and in fact are part of the design. In this way, I hope that you will find the class activities to be pragmatically useful as you explore your given career path.

13. Global Citizenship: The world has become a smaller place. No longer do the oceans and mountains isolate us from the rest of the world. As the current financial crisis demonstrates, the ripple effects of economic downturns can readily circle the planet. As students and citizens, we need to be more aware of the impact that our personal actions can have, not only on our global neighbors, but also on the planet which sustains us. We face ever increasing perils in climate, poverty, famine, pandemics, pollution, nuclear proliferation, and outright war, just to name a few. In order to address these problems effectively, we must view ourselves as stewards of the planet, each of us holding ourselves responsible for the impacts we make. This starts with our families, neighbors, and communities. But the prerequisite for this awareness is for each individual to engage in a self reflective attitude which seeks to better understand the role and purpose of his/her own existence. This action is the fundamental first step in seeking to better understand our relationship to ourselves and others. It may be difficult to question our assumptions and values, especially in a culture that values self determination and expression. It may be a path less taken by most, but if sufficient courage is mustered for this type of self discovery, it may reap dividends for the self and for those the self encounters. One can only imagine the effect of a critical mass of self reflectors on the state of global affairs. It is reasonable to infer that such persons would be more willing to listen, to understand, to empathize, and less willing to jump to conclusions, and to pre-judge.

    To better understand our relationships to others and the environment, we need to become open to consideration of perspectives which may be very different from our own. In essence, we must develop an active awareness that we have a self limited perspective on the world. Think of this as a way of stretching your conscious awareness of other ways to look at things. When you consider multiple primary and secondary perspectives (points of view) in a presentation case, you are stretching your consciousness in this way. It is the practiced development of this awareness that eventually blossoms into a true intellectual empathy for others and for the planet.

14. For Goodness Sake: The third part of the Paul-Elder model for critical thinking deals with Trait development. Traits are dispositions to act in certain ways. For example, we may say that John has developed a trait of being timely; or Betty has a trait of being honest; Mike may have developed the trait of duplicity, and so on. Note that not all traits are necessarily positive. There is a long standing developmental argument as to whether traits are innately acquired through gene inheritance, or whether environmental factors are more influential. Undoubtedly, both factors play an important role. The genetic part may largely be out of our control, but we can have a significant effect over environmental and developmental factors.

   The ancient Greeks had a belief that "habits build character" over time. That is, the type of things we do on a day to day basis influence our development. It is a corollary to the notion that "we are what we eat". In this manner, we may very well become what we think about over time.

   As we consider the traits mentioned in the last portion of the Paul-Elder booklet, the traits of intellectual courage, persistence, empathy, integrity, fairmindedness, humility, autonomy, and confidence in reason, we may wonder how they might be achieved? We may also wonder what the world would look like it most people possessed these traits. Clearly, it would be a much different place than what we too often see in the news media. The willful harming of another's property or their lives in not a sign of empathy, the lack of commitment of a parents support of their children is not integrity, failure to speak up when someone is unjustly harmed or humiliated is not intellectual courage, and an attitude of giving up too easily is not persistence. How can we have more of the positive traits and fewer of the negative traits exhibited in a given society? If we assume that the ancient Greeks were correct, then we can reasonably infer that our thoughts and actions are intricately related. That what we think does eventually influence our actions, and that changing behavior means fundamentally changing not only what we think, but how we think. There is no illusion that one college course, or even a degree's worth of courses, will guarantee the establishment of positive traits in an educated populace. This is the work of a lifetime, that each individual will have to pursue at his/her own pace. For various reasons, some will never fully achieve these virtuous traits. But even if only a small minority do, the impact of such persons on the world can be dramatic. I am hopeful that many of you will take up this challenge, and seek to develop such traits that have made so much difference to the human condition over the centuries.

Finally, to paraphrase something that John F. Kennedy said at the time he gave the nation a vision for landing on the Moon within the decade of the 1960's: "We don't do this because it is easy, we do it because it is hard". Only through the struggle of overcoming obstacles to your education, only by the self discipline that comes with setting goals, only by the persistence of practice, and the integrity of staying commited to quality standards will you succeed in your efforts. Do not avoid the resistance and the struggle. Just like muscles, the brain needs resistance to make it stronger. I hope that this class can provide you the proper degree of useful resistance that will challenge and motivate you to reach your full potential. Good luck in your struggle, and try to have some fun along the way!

"Prejudices, it is well known, are most difficult to eradicate from the heart whose soil has never been loosened or fertilized by education."   – Charlotte Bronte

Chapter 1: The Thinking Process Applied to Law-Legal Briefing

If there is a buzz word for the new century in Education, is it likely to be Assessment. In times of scarcity of resources it is no wonder the public, through its elected officials, seek to hold its institutions more accountable for the products or services they provide to society. This is no easy task when one considers the intangible "product" that education assists in producing. The necessary prerequisite for this grand task, of course, is to determine a mechanism for the quantification of such an abstract endeavor. Is it possible to measure, with some level of accuracy, what is being accomplished in the minds of students? If so, how do we formulate a system of measurement that is relatively standardized across disciplines? Do we focus on the content/substantive side of education, or do we look to cognitive processes which transcend content. The answers to what should be taught, what product is produced, and how limited resources should be allocated to achieve our intentions are ultimately both philosophical and economic questions.

This is a task that has challenged many institutions and departments. Many have labored to produce their own versions of learning outcomes expected of graduates. There is a remarkable similarity among such descriptors; quantitative reasoning, writing, responsibility, oral communication, aesthetic and multicultural awareness, and, of course the ubiquitous critical thinking.

By use of such descriptors, it is apparent that most campuses have chosen the process side of the equation to quantify. Implied by selection of these descriptors is the notion of similarity in processing skills among disparate campus departments. Nonetheless, there is a price to be paid for turning our attention to cognitive processes and attempting to make them transparent. This economic decision invariably requires sacrificing the opportunity to cover content in exchange for the time and energy devoted to process. Only individual faculty members can strike that philosophical balance.

Through time, experience, and reflection this author has concluded that process should be a major focus of attention in undergraduate courses, and that assisting students achieve their full potential through continuous improvement is the larger purpose. The implication clearly being that fully actualized persons not only makes good workers, but better neighbors and citizens as well. To the extent that content suffers, it is hoped that the process skills gained will more than compensate for any informational deficits.

Central to the focus on learning process, is a system of thought that is not only conducive to assessment, but also one which can assist in development of broad based skills. Ideally, such a system could cut across disciplines and be conducive to real world functions. A model utilized to achieve this function at a growing number of institutions is the Paul-Elder critical thinking model.[1] This model entails three distinct aspects which I refer to as: Logical Analysis, Objective Assessment, and Trait Development. The applicability of this theoretical construct to the teaching and learning of legal subject matter can be very relevant and effective, particularly to the case method approach to learning.

Informal Logical Analysis:

The term used in the context of this text is not to be confused with formal logic. The Paul-Elder version is more accurately described as a clearly informal system, which may be applied to any cognitive endeavor. Simply stated, this phase of the construct consists of breaking thinking down into its component parts, and endeavoring to reflect on each. This self reflective, or metacognitive step, assists the student to appreciate that: (a) thinking has component parts, whether we realize it or not, and (b) reflecting on such parts provides insights into flaws which may exist in such thought, or the relative quality of such thought. In short, it helps tell the student "what" their minds are doing.

Objective Assessment:

The first phase, above, is insufficient to tell the student "how" well their minds are functioning. For this aspect, a set of standards more or less capable of uniform acceptance are necessary to evaluate the quality of thought, or the products emanating therefrom. The phase of "objective assessment" fills that need. The term "objective" is a fundamental principle to any law student, but is also critical to the appreciation of its importance in assessment activities. It is only when agreed upon standards of assessment are used to value student work that such assessment provides meaningful data as to the quality of a student's cognitive processes.

Trait Development:

The ancient Greeks fully understood that habit builds character. We tend to become increasingly proficient in what we do and practice over time. Eventually, this becomes a part of who we are, and certain traits tend to emerge. Certain dispositions, and eventually character, is built over time from the stones of habitual patterns of thought, emotion, and action. In the classical Aristotelian view, logos (logic) combined with pathos (passion) eventually contributes to and becomes Ethos (character) over time. This may help us appreciate the underlying meaning of "ethics" in general.

Relevance to the Study of Law: The Case Method

The Analytic Phase:

As legal professionals know, the case method approach is historically rooted in most law based curriculums. This approach is entirely consistent with the logical analysis described above. Below is a comparison between generalized logical analysis, and legal case analysis:

Generic Analysis	Legal Analysis
1. Information	1. Facts of a dispute/conflict
2. Point of View	2. Disparate views of plaintiff v. defendant (secondary pov's are also common)

3. Questions	3. Legal Issues created
4. Concepts	4. Legal Rules, principles, codes, laws, or precedent
5. Interpretation	5. Legal Reasoning-applying the concept to the facts in order to answer the legal question.
6. Implications/Consequences	6. Precedent value of the case

It should be noted here, that there are two further elements in generic logical analysis, those of Purpose and Assumptions. These continue to exist in Legal Analysis. However, they remain largely silent elements, as the purpose of the legal system is always to resolve central disputes in a civilized manner, and the assumption is generally that the outcome will be just and equitable. While always subject to challenge, there is no need to reiterate these components in every case.

A group might argue, for example, that they believe justice was <u>not</u> done in a particular case. If they take this position, however, they should be prepared to give their rationale. They might even have a disagreement within the members of their group, in which case they could present both sides of the argument. Just because a court decided a case in a particular way does not mean a group has to agree with it, but it does mean they should have a reasonable basis for their disagreement.

The Paul-Elder logic wheel is circular as to suggest that there is no starting or ending point in the analytic process, one can start at any point on the wheel. Nonetheless, it is sometimes more efficient to sequence the elements in a particular manner, so as to create a systematic and clear flow in a presentation. As with music, sometimes it is better to play a song in a particular key! In order to facilitate better organization of case presentations, therefore, I suggest the following sequence:

1. Facts or Information- Who are the parties, what happened, where it happened, what are the timelines, etc. If the case was originally heard in a lower court, what did the original trail court decide?
2. Points of View- What are the party's biases? How do they look at the situation? Are there secondary relevant points of view, such as economic, political, historical, cultural, ethical, social, etc? Numerous points of view add to the "breadth" of a presentation.
3. Issue: What is the main question or problem the court is trying to resolve? If there are several issues, which is or are the most important or significant?
4. Concepts: What are the laws, statutes, principles, rules, or codes that can be applied to the case? Which are most relevant?
5. Interpretation, inferences and conclusion: This is the reasoning step. Students will need to discuss how the court <u>applied the relevant concept to the underlying factual information in order to resolve the question or main issue in the case.</u> What is the main conclusion the court reached?

6. Implication or consequences: This is answering the "so what?" question. What difference might this case make in the future or, if a case is an older one, what consequences flowed from this decision? In other words, what might similarly situated parties do <u>differently</u> in the future because of the ruling in this case, or what actual changes happened in society because of this case? By considering this logical element, students gain an appreciation of a case's precedent value. This may require more fact gathering to discover, but one might find ample additional information on the internet. In so doing, a group can add to the depth of a case presentation.

It is hoped that each group considers their presentation as an opportunity to develop the mental skills of organization, clarity, and communication, and to appreciate the realization that to communicate well is to think well.

The object of each presentation then becomes: to understand that case's essential logic. When that is accomplished, then any additional information generally leads to depth of understanding. Whereas, if the essential logic of a case in not comprehended, additional information often simply leads to student confusion.

The Assessment Phase:

Performing the essential briefing of a legal case, in the manner described above, helps guide the students in "what they are doing", but does not give them an indication of "how well they are doing it". This second important aspect requires a mechanism of measurement against agreed upon standards of intellectual endeavor. Naturally, to be most effective and workable, such standards must be objective in nature, such that most persons could agree with them. According to the Paul Elder Model, elements of thought are finite, but standards can be varied in number according the context of the required cognitive tasks.

In general, the most common standards which are applicable to an Introductory or Business Law class are: Clarity, Accuracy, Logic, Relevance, Depth, Breadth, Significance, and Fairness. *Refer to Appendix: Elaboration of Scoring Guidelines* which provides a definition for the above standards, along with a grading rubric for assessing the quality of a case presentation.

Some faculty might choose to allow a level of peer student evaluation based upon these standards as a vehicle for greater appreciation for what the standards actually mean in the real world, and for their own pending presentations.

At the conclusion of a case analysis or briefing in this manner, it is hoped that students will not only attain a sense of appreciation for the nature and development of the law, but also of their own abilities to achieve a level of cognitive complexity equal to the task. For this purpose, I find it useful to map out a hierarchical structure for students to ponder.

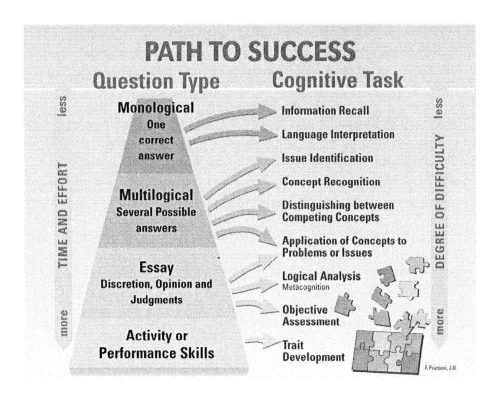

This Time-Energy Pyramid is useful in conveying the following inferences:

1. There is a correlation between time and energy expended on a cognitive task and the cognitive skills developed thereby. A useful analogy in this regard is that of a fitness center. One can not expect "6 pack abs" by standing around watching others work out. The clear implication being that there is no free lunch in cognitive skill development.

2. A natural progression of skills are required as prerequisites to achieving more advanced skills. In this respect, this is a modification or extrapolation of the classic notion in Bloom's taxonomy, although there are conceptual differences in terminology.
3. A conceptual map can be useful in identifying, not only where a student might be in his or her cognitive development, i.e., self assessment, but also some end point to aspire to. It should be noted, for example, that the "logical analysis" referred to above is quite far down in the Time-Energy pyramid. It is also important to recognize that the end point of trait development is the work of a lifetime, and may never be fully achieved. This idea may be akin to Carl Roger's classic notion of "self actualization" or achieving one's full human potential. In legal terms, this is entirely consistent with the notion of the fictitious "reasonable person" standard. We can aspire to be this person, but no one ever achieves it at all times. In other words, effort and practice are required to overcome natural tendencies of poor thinking habits.

Group Dynamics:

The familiar case method approach provides a useful and relevant vehicle for accomplishing the broad based objectives outlined above. In addition, it transfers some of the responsibility for learning to the students themselves. An increasing number of studies have demonstrated the positive effect that group learning can have on individual learners.[2]

In this respect, a group learning activity of this sort can become an avenue for exploration of a laissez-faire economic model, where students might be guided as to what to produce, but have freedom in attempting to determine and allocating their resources efficiently. Ideally, the intellectual product they produce can set a competitive standard for subsequent groups to emulate, or attempt to surpass. Anecdotal observation suggests that this has an effect on stimulating intellectual curiosity and motivation unlikely to be duplicated in traditional lecture formats.

Notwithstanding the above, the reality of group dynamics can have a tempering effect on the lofty aspirations that some groups may have. This is especially the case, when we add the cultural and language challenges attributable to ever increasing classroom diversity. Challenges such as this, may create disincentives for students and faculty alike to engage in such activities, as more time and energy must be devoted to management of group tasks. This makes it critical to clearly set out the theoretical basis, purpose and underlying philosophy for such intended endeavors. In other words, students are more apt to buy into the group tasks if they can appreciate the likelihood that greater personal skills may develop from engaging in them. Nonetheless, group problems do arise and need to be managed in a way that not only restores functional group dynamics, but also relates to learning objectives for the class as a whole. This is particularly relevant to a law class which is fundamentally concerned with conflict resolution. The realization that conflicts potentially arising within work groups are a microcosm for appreciating the larger world of conflict resolution can be insightful. From such a standpoint, students are challenged not only to continually assess their group dynamics. (*See Appendix: "Centripetal Forces in Group Dynamics"*), but also to view problems in group dynamics as opportunities to practice skills of conflict resolution. In so doing, the relevance of this activity to law, in general, may be appreciated, and can therefore become meaningful.

In recognition of the potential for unequal individual contribution within case presentation groups, systems may be put in place which mimic the realities of authentic work experiences. Incentives can thereby be created which offer opportunities for an appreciation of how "social engineering" can be accomplished through legal, and related economic principles. In the author's class we start with the assumption of equal participation among group members. Such presumption can only be overcome at the insistence of a majority of the affected group members. Students are instructed to deal with minor issues of division of labor and participation by engaging in negotiation. For situations which are not amenable to negotiation, the legal principle of due process dictates that Notice and an Opportunity to be heard is provided to a deficient group member before any detrimental action is taken. A remediation period is then given the perceived delinquent group member, to make amends for his/her unsatisfactory performance. If this can not be achieved satisfactorily, then points may be taken away from the offending group member. In all such cases the average score for the group presentation will remain the same. That is, if some group members gain points, others will lose points. For example, in a group of 4 students scoring a 90% on a particular presentation, if the majority of the group determines that 3 members deserve 5 extra points each, then the offending member's score shall be reduced by 15% points. In the event there is a challenge to this adjustment, the offending party may petition the faculty member for a review of the matter. However, "administrative costs" in terms of points may apply as instructor time is spent to assist with either mediation (5%) or arbitration (10%). If the affected student challenges the result, they must "show reasonable cause" as to why the adjustment should not be made. In extreme cases, a majority of the group may call for a group member to be terminated from the group entirely. Thus, the affected student may risk becoming a "free agent", and may seek to be transferred to another group which is agreeable to take him or her. As this also represents a failure of group cohesion, there is a group penalty of 5% as well. The student's given track record in this instance, may not make them a desirable candidate for this option, as no group is bound to accept the affected student. In this manner, it is hoped that students will see a real world connection to their group work tasks. *Refer to Appendix: Class Rules worksheet*.

Group Presentations: Mechanism for Appeal:

One of the hallmarks of our legal system is the underlying recognition that human law making and interpretation may be flawed. This realization implies the need for a system of appeals, in which erroneously decided cases may be overturned. In keeping with this legal characteristic, a system for appealing a group presentation score is likewise available to each group, if there is a reasonable basis for doing so. Because real world appeals carry inherent risks, authentic course design suggests that similar risks be built into group work appeals. Since group presentation scores are generally given as immediately as possible following a presentation, an appeal may require added scrutiny of the presentation. This carries the risk of the final score being either higher or lower that the initial grade. Additionally, in order to deter frivolous appeals, each group must post a 5 point "bond" that is sacrificed should the faculty member determine that the appeal is frivolous on the merits. Consequently, a group considering an appeal has an incentive to perform a cost vs. benefit assessment before availing themselves of an appeal option. *Refer to Appendix: Appeal De Novo Rules*.

When viewed as a system of thinking, introductory or business law classes can be presented as process driven learning environments where students engage in authentic activities representative of real world experiences. In this manner emphasis is shifted from content driven activities such as information recall, language interpretation and issues/concept identification to higher level learning activities such as logical analysis, objective assessment, and trait development. In so doing, students may gain a better appreciation that higher level thinking skills can be used in a myriad of diverse subject areas, academic or otherwise. In this manner barriers which artificially separate learning into discreet content areas are made more porous, and bridges are built between content areas and the world in general. Anecdotal evidence suggests that students appreciate and feel empowered by these experiences. As students learn to better assess their own thinking and learning, we can hypothesize that student skill and self efficacy are thereby improved. Further research in this area may be warranted to determine the extent and degree of such changes.

References:

1. Paul, Richard, Ph. D Critical Thinking, How to Prepare Students for a Rapidly Changing World, Foundation for Critical Thinking, 1993.

2. Ballentine, J. and Larres, P. Final Year accounting undergraduates attitudes to group assessment and the role of learning logs. Accounting Education, 16(2), 163-183 (2007).

3. Van Gelder, Tim, Ph. D, "Teaching Critical Thinking, Some Lessons from Cognitive Science", College Teaching, Vol 53 no 1, 2005.

4. Baker and Campbell, "When there is Strength in Numbers, A Study of Undergraduate Task Groups", College Teaching, Vol 53, No 1, 2005.

5. Ericcson & Charness, "Cultivating Expertise in Informal Reasoning", American Psychologist 49, 725-47 (1994).

6. Wiggins, Grant, Ph. D. Educative Assessement, John Wiley and Sons, 1998.

7. Pintrich and Schunk, Motivation in Education; Theory, Research, and Applications, Prentice Hall, 1996.

8. Zachary Karabell, Ph. D. What's College For?, The Struggle to Define American Higher Education, Basic Books, Perseus Group, 1998.

9. Palomba and Banta, Assessment Essentials, Planning, Implementing and Improving Assessment in Higher Education, Jossey-Bass, 1999.

10. Logan, Frank, Fundamentals of Learning and Motivation, 2ed., William Brown and Co, 1976.

11. Paul, R., "The State of Critical Thinking Today", New Directions for Community Colleges, No. 130, Summer 2005, Wiley Periodicals, Inc.

12. Rogers, Carl. (1961). *On becoming a person: A therapist's view of psychotherapy*. London: Constable.

Chapter 2: Substantive Law: The Historical Context

Natural Law or Reason: Which Path to Justice?

Justice is not the purpose of law, but an elusive aspiration of it. Indeed, the existence of a built in appeals process in most legal systems implies the transient nature of what is considered fair and equitable at any particular time. We have learned from history, that what seemed just at one point in time, may later appear unjust. For example, the sanctioning of slavery, indentured servitude, or the subservient status of women was at one time considered part of the natural order. We now have a rather different view. The law, as a reflection of the society in which it operates, has the capacity for progressive development.

Given the above, how do we best move toward an increased probability of attaining this mystical state of equity? Such questions often depend upon ones perspective in viewing the fundamental nature of justice. Do we see it as a static notion, fixed in time by a higher intelligence, or an evolving state of being and understanding that seeks, but never quite attains, all the fruits of its potential?

If viewed pragmatically, one could assert the justice is the result of the making of good laws coupled with a fair process of enforcing them. That is, the quality of substantive law coupled with a fair process is the most likely avenue to a just result. Just like good quality materials coupled with good craftsmanship are the makings of excellent furniture, so it is with law. Nonetheless, the admonition of Bismarck should still be heeded: "One who enjoys sausage and respects the law, should watch neither being made"! It can, of course, be a quite messy process. In the news, we find many examples of the necessary political compromises required to make legislation. Sometimes, a bit of sawdust may even find its way into the political "sausage". Or to put it another way, corruption is a reality that can never be overlooked. It is the rust of political and legal systems. Legal systems, like any structure of civilization, require periodic maintenance and upkeep to keep them functioning properly. As I write this chapter, we hear news of the Obama administration wishing to reform legal regulations in order to prevent the reoccurrence of recent banking and investment failures. Only history will tell how effective these potential reforms will be.

The making of Substantive Law:

The laws of any society speak volumes about its cultural, moral, and political values. Who is best suited to make laws? And by what mechanism? The easy answer is to defer to history and tradition, the underlying assumption of which is to give credence and weight to generations of honored belief systems. These belief systems eventually become codified, or imbedded, into law. How could millennia of human experience be wrong? This is where morality or ethics through faith becomes relevant. Faith, in history and ethical mores, does not hesitate to conclude and support moral traditions. Faith does not wring its hands over contemplation of diverse perspectives and issues. Faith produces quick and efficient conviction of beliefs. In short, true faith does not question. After all, the matter is already settled by years of traditional acceptance. Justice is done because our historical traditions tell us so. Justice is something to be dispensed from a higher authority or supreme being. Such followers dare not doubt, for to do so demonstrates human arrogance and lack of reverence for supreme or revered historical authorities. This is the sentiment expressed through the underlying philosophy of "Natural Law". Justice, in this view, is not something that we can always quantify and perceive, for only the dispenser of historical wisdom has the capacity to fully appreciate its nature. It is not surprising that this philosophy held great sway, when literacy rates were extremely low and most knowledge was held by the very few, usually clergy, or nobles who could afford to be educated, had a monopoly on most information sources, and could decipher its meaning. The role of the average follower was simply to obey and follow in the hope that they too would someday understand. While this view is embodied in the Western notion of natural law, it has attained its full fruition in Islamic states where Sha'ria law is often the cornerstone of its legal systems. Sha'ria law is not in itself Muslim law, but is embedded in a religious and cultural history going back centuries. In its fullest form, Sha'rai law regulates every part of life, including some private aspects. It is generally viewed to be incompatible with democratic principles, as the will of the people is superseded by largely religious doctrines. Another item in the current news reflects this dichotomy, the current unrest over the Iranian elections. Protestors are in the streets demanding to be heard, while the Religious clerics, who hold the true power, decide which path is more compatible with their Theocratic ideals.

Law by reason provides an alternative route to possible justice. While the pathway of faith appears paved, straight, and obstacle free, the path of reason is rutted and meandering, sometimes circling back upon itself until it straightens again for a time. It is a path filled with obstacles which distract and deter us from our goals. It requires of the traveler skill, perseverance, confidence, humility, and integrity of principle. While faith abhors doubt and deters questioning, the path of reason requires it. Indeed without questioning the traveler can not sustain his/her journey. As a contrast to Sha'ria law, it is more compatible with democratic principles of self governance, yet its propensity for error and imperfection is embedded into its structure. For example, the appeal process is a recognition that courts can, and sometimes do, fail to reach a just and fair result. Sometimes several appeals may be necessary to reach what is perceived to be a "just" conclusion. Even then, history may ultimately prove the decision to be much less just than it appeared at the time. Cases like <u>Dred Scott vs. Sandford, Plessy v. Ferguson</u>, and the Supreme Court's overturning of the National Recovery Act in 1934 are good examples of what could be described as the "illusion of justice".

To summarize the above, it can be said that what society perceives as "law" is both culturally dependent and evolving over time. Consider the Venn Diagram of Law vs. Morality below. This illustration depicts the idea that, although there is a distinction between laws and morals, there is also a degree of overlap that, in the Western view, is dynamically changing over time. Further clarification is provided by considering the examples within each portion of the diagram. Essentially, these two realms of law and morality address fundamentally different questions. While morality or ethics is primarily concerned with how we **should** live, law addresses how we **must** live (in order to avoid legal sanction or punishment). Of course, we keep in mind higher ideals as we live our day to day lives, but in the meantime, there are disputes and disagreements to be settled (hopefully in a fair manner).

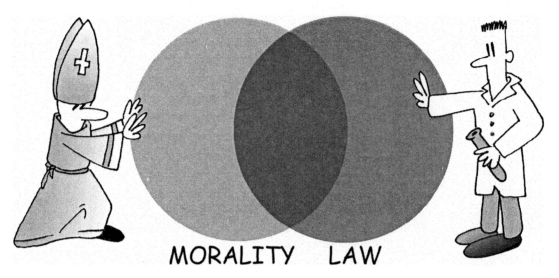

Law vs. Morality- United States

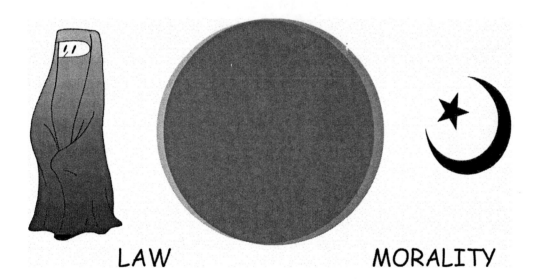

Law vs. Morality- Parts of Middle East (Theocratic societies)

The degree of overlap of these 2 realms is <u>culturally dependent, and dyanmic over time.</u>

Ch. 2: Group Work Exercise: Compare and Contrast

1. *Think of and describe further example of similarities and differences between law and morality.*

2. *What sorts of things might fit in the "overlap area"? Provide specific examples.*

3. *Give historical examples of how the degree of overlap has changed over time. Do you think it is changing today? What trend do you see? Give examples.*

4. *Keeping in mind the above frame of reference, discuss what is meant by "Justice"? Provide examples where you feel justice was or was not done. What factors affect the outcome?*

5. *Given the following scenario, argue for justice from the frame of reference of Sha'ria law, as opposed to Common Law. Note: You may need to argue from a philosophical viewpoint, unless you can cite specific concepts of justice in each system.*

   An extremely thin runway model is prohibited from participating in a fashion show due to being below guidelines for height and weight. State regulations are aimed at reducing the incidence of eating disorders, such as bulimia, from becoming more prominent among young girls who tend to emulate the appearance of fashion models. A very thin model who is prevented from participating in the show challenges the regulation. Should she prevail and be allowed to participate irrespective of her weight?

   (As you analyze the above question from each viewpoint, consider whether this is primarily a moral or legal problem or has aspects of both? Where do legal, or moral principles comes from in each instance, who is in the best position to decide? What are the social-cultural influences that affect interpretation of these laws or principles over time?)

The Roots of the US Legal System:

A quirk of geography was fundamental to the development of the Law of the United States. In 410 A.D. the Romans withdrew from Britain after nearly 400 years of colonization. The Effect of this was to essentially leave the local British tribes; the Celts, Scotts, Welsh, Druids, Angles, Saxons etc to themselves. Building upon some of the Roman principles of law, the locals began to experiment with various mechanisms for dispute resolution. In 1066 A.D., The Norman, William the Conqueror defeated and killed the then Anglo-Saxon King Harold at the Battle of Hastings. In order to maintain control of his new country he established basic principles of feudalism, remnants of which still exist today. A more complete History of the evolution of the Common Law can be found on my instructor website.[1,2] Naturally, as children of our British ancestors, the United States adopted many of the principles and practices of this Common Law history, but without resort to the historical privileges of the nobility.

In summary, two basic components of this legal evolution were the Courts of the Exchequer for the purpose of tax and money issues, and the Courts of the Chancery, for matters of "equity" or court ordered sanctions. Over time, these two court systems merged into one basic system, but these two separate forms of remedies still exist today. Modern examples of equitable remedies include; specific performance, injunctions, dissolution decrees, rescission of contracts, and orders of child support.

Don't worry...we got this in the bag! They'll just have you jump off the cliff and when you go "splat" on the ground, that'll prove that you are not a witch!

Trying to Find Justice:
Trial by Ordeal

As dispute resolution became more complex and legal rulings began to become more centralized, it became increasingly important for some semblance of consistency to emerge from the courts. Courts began to experiment with various forms of trial as well, the corner stone of which was to attempt to get at the best approximation of the "truth", these included some rather brutal notions such as trial by ordeal or battle. One favored form was to toss alleged criminal into water on the theory that god would determine who was guilty or innocent.

The trial by ordeal method eventually lost favor, and was officially banned in 1215 A.D., the same year of the signing of the **Magna Carta**.

After this period of "experimentation", Courts began to look at the way similar cases had been decided by other courts. Thus, the concept of **Stare Decisis** (to stand by prior decisions**,** or the idea of **precedent** came into being. The basic principle is that similar cases should be decided in a similar fashion, and that the laws should be applied in a consistent fashion among cases with the same factual pattern.

<u>Legal Structure</u>:

If we think of the legal system as a building, then we could imagine that the foundation for such building would be based upon the Common Law tradition discussed above. As was the case with churches being built upon the foundation of previous temples, so the U.S. legal system has been built upon the ancient common law framework.

In the United States, we have continued to build upon this common law foundation, by creating new law in various forms: Legislation passed by Congress, Executive Orders promulgated by the Executive (President), Treaties between nations, Model Codes, Regulations by both Executive and Legislative branch agencies, and a continuation of the Common law as decided on a case by case basis.

Of course, every sustainable structure requires a room to hold and protect the contents of any structure. In our system, this function is represented by the U.S. Constitution. We are the first government ever to have established a Constitution as the centerpiece to a system of government. Any underlying law, treaty, or regulation that is not in keeping with Constitutional principles, is declared "unconstitutional" as is rendered void as a matter of law. That is, unless and until the Constitution is Amended in such a way as to allow for it.

Not surprisingly, amendments to the Constitution were made intentionally difficult by the framers of that important document. First, a supermajority of Congress must vote to propose the amendment, and then three quarters of the States must ratify the proposal within seven years of its proposal or the proposal dies. Consequently, there have been only 17 Amendments to the Constitution, since the initial ten or "Bill of Rights" were adopted in 1791.

Amending the Constitution

As illustrated above, you will note the spaces between the legal pillars. Sometimes there are legal issues that emerge for which there is no specific modern day statute, regulation, or rule. In these areas of law, sometime an old principle of the Common Law can still be used, and applied, to resolve a current dispute. In this respect, the Common law foundation can also provide a "safety net" of legal concepts which are still applicable today. Hint: These old common law doctrines still retain their original Latin names. For example, "caveat emptor" (let the buyer beware) and "res ipsa loquitor" (the act speaks for itself) are still principles which can be applied today. Legal areas like contract law or trusts are filled with these ancient, but still relevant doctrines.

Also note the reference to the "50 mini-me" models in the upper right corner. This is a reference to the fact that we have 50 states which form the same basic structure of government, albeit on a smaller scale.

A Hierarchy of Laws:

Not all laws are created equal in terms of their scope or potential effect. Some law are subservient to higher laws, so there is a pecking order to determine which laws shall govern in the event of conflict. In essence, this is a legal version of the "big fish eat little fish" scenario, which all has to do with the concept of Power or **Jurisdiction**. Literally translated the term jurisdiction means "to speak the law", or more accurately, the power to speak the law.

In its most simple form, power is nothing more than having the ability to make someone do what they don't really want to do. In this respect, there are two fundamental forms of power, legitimate and illegitimate. One who brandishes a firearm in order to get what he/she wants is exhibiting a very illegitimate form of power. Our studies will not directly deal with area, with the possible exception of the criminal law chapter. We are concerned with legitimate forms of power which are fundamentally derived from the consent of the governed. In other words, it is the type of power that is expressly or impliedly authorized by a government of the people, by and through their legal representatives. We keep in mind, however, that no power is absolute. Therefore, one must first determine the nature and scope of any legitimate power that exists before dealing with the merits of a particular dispute. The study of Jurisdiction is the study of the nature and limits of such power, and is the first issue that must be addressed in any dispute resolution system. A court can do nothing until it first has the authorized and legitimate power to do so. There are two fundamental different forms of legal power. First, the courts must have legitimate power over the subject matter of the dispute. Second, they must also have legitimate power over the parties to the dispute. Here we begin with another diagram:

Subject Matter Jurisdiction:

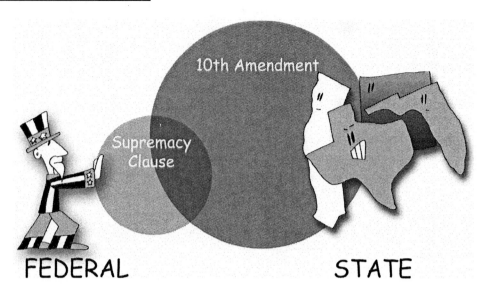

The above diagram is a pictorial representation of the natural tension that exists in the U.S. Constitution between the Supremacy Clause in the Constitution and the 10th Amendment. The supremacy clause indicates that Federal Law is supreme over the states, but only if such power is **enumerated** or listed in the Constitution. We will see later that the U.S. Supreme Court has some important leeway to determine whether such power can also be implied. Several important historical cases has so held.[3]

The counterforce to the Supremacy Clause is the 10 Amendment, which provides that all power not given to the Federal Government by the Constitution is "reserved to the States, or to the people". Thus, the province of State Power typically applies to **health, safety and welfare issues,** for which the Supreme court of a particular state has final authority! In the above illustration, the State circle is larger to depict a greater scope of cases in this area.

Notwithstanidng the above, is an area of overlap between Federal and State power, known as **Concurrent Jurisdiction**, or the area of shared power. Cases in this area are of two varieties:

1. Federal Question cases: A federal question is an issue that emanates from the Constitution, laws (statutes), or treaties of the United States.
2. Diversity of Jurisdiction: These cases deal with parties from different states, or countries, but only in the case where the dollar amount in controversy is reasonably alleged to exceed $75,000.

In both of the above instances, an aggrieved party (the plaintiff) may <u>choose</u> to take the matter to either Federal Court or State Court, depending on where they think they will get the best result. This is sometimes referred to as "forum shopping", but in reality there are strict limits in determining this.

Another important difference is in the laws that apply to federal question vs. diversity cases. In federal question cases, only federal law applies, whereas in diversity cases, the courts will apply the law of the <u>State</u> which has the closest connection to the disputed transaction.[4] In other words, in diversity cases, the courts apply state substantive law, but federal procedure!

<u>Jurisdiction Over the Parties</u>:

In addition to having power over the subject matter of the dispute, courts must still have power over the adversary parties, or their property. This is the second necessary form of jurisdiction, and has three separate forms: In Rem (power over property or things within a state); Over the Persons within a state (usually where the defendant resides, or by long arm jurisdiction if out of state); and "quasi in rem" or attachment jurisdiction which allows for courts to attach a defendant's property in order to enforce a personal obligation.

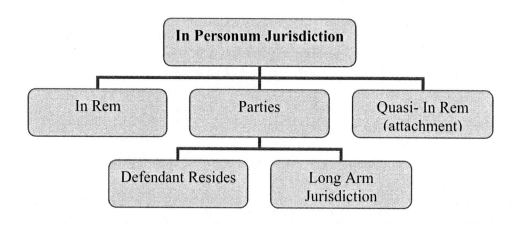

An example of in Rem jurisdiction would be a dispute about property boundaries between neighbors. If the land or property lies within the boundaries of State X, then that state is said to have in Rem jurisdiction to decide the matter. By the same token, if a dispute is about something a person did in a state, then the State where the defendant resides, or where the conduct occurred has jurisdiction to decide the case. The variation of Long-Jurisdiction applies if a person or business entity has engaged in business, committed a crime or tort, signed a contract, owns property in a state if that property is the subject of the dispute. This provision allows for states to exercise some power over non-residents if they have had the requisite "minimum contacts" with the State in question.[5]

Finally, in quasi in rem or 'attachment' jurisdiction, the court can take control of a person's obligation by seizing property which can then be sold to pay on a plaintiff's claim. For example, if one were to obtain a court judgment that a party owes him $5,000, but the defendant has no means to pay, the court could issue a writ of attachment to seize and sell the vehicle to pay the underlying judgment.

References:

1. Instructor website: www.instruction.greenriver.edu/fprimiani
2. A brief History of the Common Law (Early History) http://www.luyulei.cn/case_law?1-1CommonLawHistory.htm
3. *Gibbons v. Ogden*, 22 U.S. 1 (1824), was a case in which the Supreme Court of the United States held that the power to regulate interstate commerce was granted to Congress by the Commerce Clause of the Constitution.
4. *Erie Railroad Co. v. Tompkins*, 304 U.S. 64 (1938), was a decision by the Supreme Court of the United States in which the Court held that federal courts did not have the power to make up general federal common law when hearing state law claims under diversity jurisdiction. In reaching this holding, the Court overturned almost a century of federal civil procedure law, and established what remains the modern law of diversity jurisdiction for United States federal courts.
5. *International Shoe Co. v. Washington*, 326 U.S. 310 (1945) was a landmark decision of the United States Supreme Court holding that a civil defendant could not be subjected to personal jurisdiction by the courts of a state unless the defendant had certain minimum contacts with that state.

21

Chapter 3: Civil Legal Procedure

<u>The Conflict Resolution Funnel:</u>

We have noted that the main purpose of our legal system, and most all legal systems worldwide, is organized, predictable and civilized dispute resolution. Heaven knows there are many "uncivilized" forms of dispute resolution, the worst of which is outright war. History has shown that such forms of attempted dispute resolution rarely achieve a mutually agreeable end result and, of course, many lives are lost in the process.

This chapter deals with how the legal system attempts to bring about fair and just resolutions in the most economically feasible manner possible. By "economic" here, recall that I mean more that just monetary interests, but also the time, talent, and energy required to achieve a just result. Viewed in this manner, it is fairly easy to see that "justice", or the best perception of it, can be an expensive, albeit intangible, commodity. Much time and energy can be spent in the pursuit of it, and there are certainly no guarantees of success in achieving it. Nonetheless, we humans persist in seeking it out.

Life is full of disputes and, as stated above, the primary function of any legal system is the civilized resolution of it. If we view conflict resolution as the core of what we call "justice", then we can consider the degree and quantity of resources we wish to expend to achieve the best approximation of it, from our individual perspectives. Of course the "homo Economicus" in all of us, wishes to expend no more resources than necessary to achieve their view of justice. Therefore, when we experience conflict we generally start with the rather inexpensive direct negotiation with the party we are in dispute with. Then, we gradually expend more time, talent, and treasure resources as is warranted to achieve our ultimate goal. Consider the diagram below, which I refer to as the "Dispute Resolution Funnel". The funnel represents the intake of any number and kind of conflicts or disputes between persons or entities of various sorts. The top portion of the funnel is where most conflicts arise, and are most cost effectively managed by **negotiation, mediation or arbitration**. These three mechanisms represent the "informal" or "alternate" forms of dispute resolution (ADR). At this point, most (surely over 95%) of legal disputes will "filter out" of the funnel by one or more of these mechanisms. The more difficult or intransigent a dispute becomes, the greater the degree of resources required to manage it, and the chances of resolving the issue by the parties alone becomes less likely.

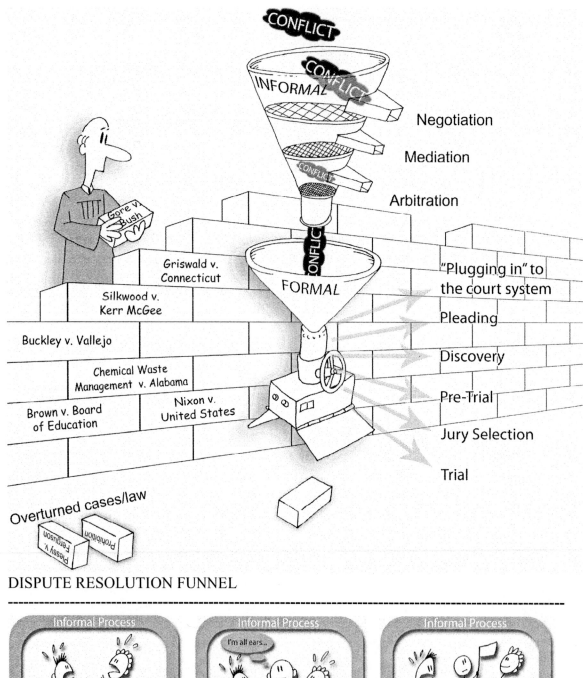

DISPUTE RESOLUTION FUNNEL

ALTERNATE DISPUTE RESOLUTION

One resource that is indispensable in bringing about resolution, is the legitimate power that can be applied to compel a resolution. Such "power of compulsion" is a fundamentally limiting resource for the primary adversarial parties. When parties reach the limits of what their negotiating prowess can influence or compel, they will need to resort to the power base of the "formal" conflict resolution mechanism of the Courts. It is interesting to note here, that the initial phase of this formal resolution process is referred to as the "**Pleading**" phase, bringing to mind an image of a person coming to court on bended knee seeking to engage the Court's power to resolve a conflict he/she has no further authority to compel.

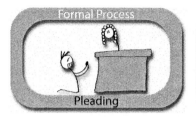
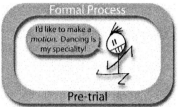

Formal Dispute Resolution:

Keep in mind, that even if the parties reach a "settlement" of their dispute informally, that written settlement document becomes enforceable only because the legal system will act to give legal effect of that settlement through long standing principles of the common law tradition. Of course, there can always be disagreement about just what the principles of such common law mean, or how and when they apply. The inherent power of the State, through the court system, in this instance becomes the ingredient that adds the sufficient seriousness to address these questions, and achieve finality of the conflict. In latin, this is referred to as the "**Res Judicata**" moment. That is, the finality of at least the factual basis of the legal dispute. Barring claims of appeal on legal grounds, that decision will forever stand, unless eventually reversed in some appeal process. As represented in the diagram, it is at this point that the case does become "another brick in the wall" of the ever changing Common Law. As each new case is decided by the courts, it becomes a potential precedent for later cases of a similar nature. The is referred to as the principle of "**stare decisis**", or standing by principles of prior decisions.

From time to time, some bricks of that wall of common law may fall by the wayside, or be replaced with newer bricks more in keeping with the changing social mores of the time. For example, even the U.S. Supreme Court case of **Plessy v. Ferguson** which was deeply embedded in our Common Law heritage for over 70 years, was eventually reversed by a 9-0 margin in the 1954 case of **Brown v. Board of Education**. It can be said that the "mortar of perceived justice" surrounding the Plessy case had given way, and was dislodged from the case made wall of common law. The Plessy case was thereby relegated to the rubble of erroneous decisions.

Stages of Formal Dispute Resolution (Civil Litigation):

In the adversary system, the person who begins formal litigation is entitled the plaintiff and the one who is defending the lawsuit is the defendant. In the pleadings phase, the process begins with the filing of a **Summons and Complaint**, which must be properly served upon the defendant in one of several properly recognized manners. The most common and effective of these is personal service. The Summons simply gives basic notice of the fact that a lawsuit has begun and instructs the Defendant as to what must be done to respond to the Complaint. If the defendant does not respond in a timely manner (typically 20 days) they will risk the entry of a **Default Judgment**, which means the plaintiff is entitled to everything they claimed in their complaint. At a minimum, the defendant should at least file a **Notice of Appearance** in order to avoid a Default without notice. The purpose of this phase of formal proceedings is simply to determine what basic facts are in dispute, and what the initial arguments of the respective adversaries are.

Next, each party must go about the process of gathering **evidence** which will support their arguments. If we think of the proverbial "scales of justice" so frequently depicted in various aspects of the media, it is evidence that is gathered by the parties in order to present to the jury for "weighing". Note that not all evidence needs be evident, that is, visible to the unaided eye. There are many forms of evidence that can not been seen, but still objectively verified and measured. This evidence, combined with the weightiness of reason may eventually be sufficient to tip the scales of justice slightly more in one direction than another. The critical degree of tipping is the so called "**preponderance of the evidence**" in a civil matter, more commonly described as the "**more likely than not**" standard of sufficiency. In a criminal matter, far more evidence is required for a conviction, the so called **"beyond a reasonable doubt"** standard.

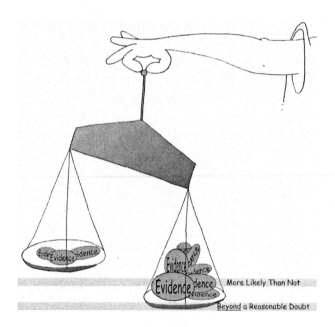

The basic premise is that all evidentiary cards should be on the table and accessible to either party, unless such evidence is privileged in some way. The specific rules of evidence are quite lengthy and technical, and beyond the scope of this book. Suffice it to say that the admissibility of evidence in a formal trial is subject to considerable scrutiny. It is also subject to a fairly strict timeline, which must be complied with under penalty of court imposed **sanctions**. During this so called **discovery** process, status conferences may occur to keep the parties on track with their investigational efforts. Mechanisms of discovery can vary, but may include **interrogatories** (written questions), **depositions** (questioning under oath), witness interviews, photographs, and even **requests for production** of evidence held by the opposing party. All such evidence must be open and available to both parties unless it is recognized by rule as being prejudicial or otherwise protected from discovery.

Tools of Administrative Efficiency:

As one can gather, the formal dispute resolution process can be quite lengthy and expensive in dollars and resources. This is true not only for the parties involved, but also for the court system as a whole. Because of the relative scarcity of resources available to resolve a growing number of cases, there has been an increasing concern for preventing needless waste of time and resources expended in formal dispute resolution. For this reason, court rules allow for motions to be made which can request the court to expedite or short circuit the resolution of disputes in given situations. Chief among them is the **Motion for Summary Judgment**, which allows either party to request a resolution to the case in the **Pre-trial** phase. Based upon the Federal Rules of Evidence, Civil Rule 56, it provides that a Judge may grant an Order for Summary Judgment if and when "there are no material issues of fact in dispute", when "viewed in the light most favorable to the non-moving party" contesting the motion. This motion makes sense when we keep in mind the disparate functions of the Judge and Jury in a civil or criminal case. That is, the Judge decides the Law, but the Juries decide the Facts. That being said, if there are no material (i.e. significant) issues of fact in dispute, then that is another way of saying that there is really nothing for a Jury to do if the case moves forward. That is, the facts are so clearly established that the case can be legally resolved by the Judge at this early stage. A case example of this is the Parker v. 20th Century Fox case. 3 Cal.3d 176, 89 Cal.Rptr. 737, 474 P.2d 689.

It may be important here to note that a trial by jury is a constitutional right under the 7th Amendment. However, it is a right that is entirely optional. There may be times when the parties do not desire their case heard by a jury. In this instance, the trial is referred to as a **"Bench Trial"**, and the Judge decides both the facts and the law. Small Claims courts, as seen on TV, are of this nature. However, even larger Superior Court cases can be of this nature, if neither adversarial party requests a jury, and pays the required fee (usually about $200).

Because Summary Judgment is such a drastic remedy in that it essentially takes away a party's Constitutional right to a jury trial, the standard is set high to obtain such a ruling. Consequently, most motions for summary judgment will fail. On the other hand, another opportunity to short circuit the case occurs after the plaintiff has finished presenting his or her case. That is, when all of the evidence and witness have been presented to the court. It is at this stage that a motion similar to summary judgment is available. The Motion for a **Directed Verdict** can be requested when one party feels that the evidence presented by the plaintiff is legally insufficient to prevail on the merits. Once again, the concern for administrative efficiency is displayed.

Finally, even after the verdict has been rendered by a jury, the opposing party may still request the Judge to overrule the juries verdict by a requesting a **Judgment Notwithstanding the verdict (JNOV)**. In other words, if it become apparent that the case has been wrongly decided by a misapplication or misperception of the law by the jury, this last option is available to prevent needless appeals.

Perhaps even more interesting than the JNOV, is its corollary, **jury nullification**. This rather unusual remedy has entitled some juries in some states to effectively disregard the legal instructions they were given by a Judge, or to otherwise disregard the law as stated. Thus far, Appellate Courts have sustained cases of jury nullification in most places where they have occurred.

Jury Selection:

There is one fundamental problem with juries, and that is that they are composed of human beings, each one of which carries his or her share of beliefs, half truths, misunderstandings, bias, and outright prejudice. Some potential jurors might be aware of these human frailties, but many may also be subconscious. They may percolate to the conscious level only by being drawn out in a questioning process called "**voir dire**", or "to speak the truth". In this manner, each party's attorney is provided an opportunity to question each potential juror in an attempt to sift out any conscious or subconscious bias.

THE PURPOSE OF VOIR DIRE

The following illustration depicts how cognitive limitations and "attribution" distortions commonly come into play as we humans experience the world around us. It is sometimes said that we do not perceive the world as it is, but as we would like it to be. These fundamental cognitive distortions are a significant hurdle for a legal system concerned with fair and impartial hearings and trials. They must be dealt with in some systematic way in order to assure that some semblance of justice is actually accomplished.

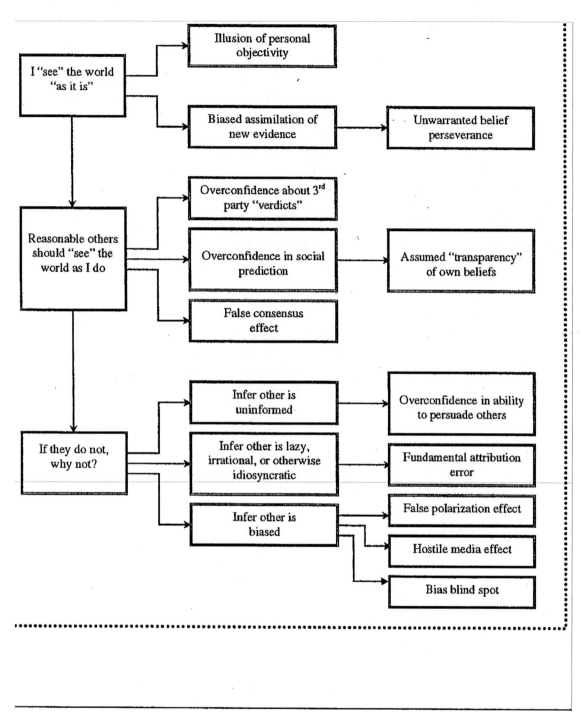

[47] This figure was adapted from a similar figure in pronin, Gilovich & Ross, *Objectivity, supra* note 53 95.

Pronin, Thomas, Gilovich and Ross, Objectivity in the Eye of the Beholder: Divergent perceptions of Bias in self versus others, 111 Psych Rev. 781 (2004).

During jury selection, therefore, if a bias or prejudice is stated outright, a **"challenge for cause"** may be made. This requests the judge to strike or reject such potential juror from serving in that particular trial. For example, if one party is representing a burn victim allegedly caused by a defendant, it would be important to know whether anyone on the jury pool has suffered a significant burn. Someone who has experienced the pain and anguish of a burn might well become biased toward the burned plaintiff by being able to sympathize with their painful injuries. Although a burned plaintiff might wish such a person on the jury, it is certain that the defense counsel would strike that juror for cause because of this likely biasing factor. There is no limit to the number of Challenges for cause a party can make.

The voir dire process also allows an opportunity for a limited number of **"peremptory challenges"** when there is no outright or blatant statement of bias or prejudice made by a potential juror. In these cases a party, through their attorney, may use this so called "wild card" challenge to excuse a juror that such party simply has a "gut instinct" or feeling about. Most jurisdictions limit these challenges to three, which must either be used or lost.

Perhaps one day, mankind will be able to set all bias and prejudices aside, or invent a less burdensome mechanism to ferret out such frailties of the human mind and heart. Until that day, however, this questioning process will likely be necessary for the foreseeable future. Like rust or corrosion, bias of the heart and mind can be an expensive commodity to eradicate, but any system that aims for justice must pay the price to see that it is eliminated or reduced to the maximum possible extent. To do otherwise, would be to fail to live up to the high standards that our forefathers, the framers, have set up for us in the world's first established Constitution.

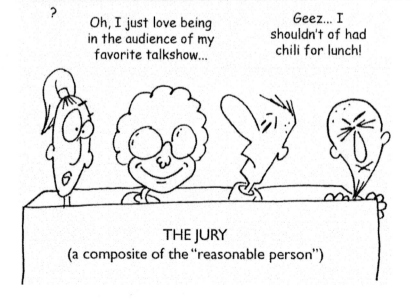

THE JURY
(a composite of the "reasonable person")

Chapter 4: Constitutional Law

A Question of Balance

In keeping with the key word theme for each chapter, the key term for this chapter is Balance. Now that we have a good idea of where law comes from and how legitimate power is achieved and recognized, we still have to contend with how it is dispersed and balanced among competing entities.

In writing the Constitution, the framers had an overriding sense of the old adage, "Absolute Power corrupts absolutely", famously stated by Lord Acton.[1] The framers wanted to divide power so that no one entity would have so much that it would become oppressive. This is the essence of the separation of powers within the branches of government. The legislative branch makes the laws, the executive branch enforces the law, and the judicial branch (the courts) interprets what the law means in individual cases. Articles 1 through 3 of the Constitution deal with the roles and powers of these branches. There was one major omission of the Constitutional Convention of 1787, and that was a Bill of Rights for the people. Though most of the State constitutions provided for these rights, the framers did not see fit to do so for the national government as a whole, besides time had pretty much run out for the convention anyway. It was not until two years after the first Congress met in 1791, that a Bill of Rights was formally passed and ratified by the States. This encompassed the first ten amendments to the Constitution, which are some of the most fundamental rights citizens enjoy.

<u>Three Dimensions of Power Balance</u>:

Virtually all Constitutional cases have to do with the Balance of this legitimate Power in what I call three separate power "Dimensions". Each Constitutional court case resolves a dispute which adjusts the balance in one or more of the following these dimensions:

Dimension 1: Balance of Power within the Government (i.e. between the branches of Government as designed in the Constitution, Executive, Legislative, and Judicial. This happens both within the Federal and State Governments, as the State systems are really a microcosm of the Federal structure. The <u>Youngstown Steel vs. Sawyer</u> case was a classic example of the struggle between President Harry S. Truman and Congress, which was decided against the president by the US Supreme court in 1952.

Dimension 2: Resolution of disputes which strike a balance between Federal vs. State Power. This concept of shared power is known as **Federalism**.
<u>Silkwood v. Kerr-McGee</u> is an example of a case in this category.

Dimension 3: As illustrated below, this area strikes a balance between Government entities of all types (federal, state, county, city, police, fire dept, etc) vs. Individual Rights. What constitutes an "individual" or "person" is an interesting subject for future discussion.[2] An example of this dimension is the <u>Gideon v. Wainright</u> case, which provided for the right of counsel to be appointed in cases where a defendant could not afford it.

Note that each of these three dimensions represents a tension between opposing extremes. In keeping with the above description, one could graph this balancing act on a three dimensional grid depicted below. The X axis (dimension 1) being the Legislative vs. Executive Power, the Y (dimension 2) axis being Federal Power vs. State Power, and the Z axis (dimension 3) being Government Power vs. Individual rights. When Constitutional cases are decided, particularly by the Supreme Court, there is a balance shift on one of more of these axes. For example, The Patriot Act passed by Congress in the aftermath of the September 11th, 2001 disaster, had the effect of shifting power toward the Executive (President) on the X axis, toward the Federal Government on the Y axis, and perhaps even toward Government and away from Individual Rights on the Z axis. While some significant cases can shift the balance one way or another to a greater degree than less significant cases, the degree of movement is not as important (for now) as simply recognizing how legislation or decided cases can shift the balance in these dimensions over time.

When important Constitutional cases come up before the U.S. Supreme Court, one can imagine the Supreme Court Justices, vested in their black robes, deliberating behind closed doors. Perhaps they are actually "tinkering" with this sort of three dimensional "gyroscope", trying to keep the entire system in overall balance?

We will see examples of cases falling into one of more of the above dimensions during the course. As you study or view some of these cases in media, be prepared to address which dimension(s) each case might fall in. Sometimes cases can begin as third dimension cases involving Government power vs. Individual rights, but end up being decided in another dimension. The infamous <u>Dred Scott v. Sanford</u> of 1857, which may well have helped lead to the Civil War was such a case. As we shall see, it began by the Scott's trying to vindicate their rights as persons. However, when the case was decided by the U.S. Supreme Court, the court upheld slavery on 2nd dimension grounds of States Rights vs. Federal Power. The Court stated that it had no power to tell the States what to do, thus insuring the outbreak of a vicious war.

"The Power of Process;
Same thinking, different implications"

Third Dimension Balancing Tests:

As stated above, Dimension 3 has to do with attempts by Government entities of all types (Fed, State, local, police, etc) to restrict or limit individual liberties, predominately found in the Amendments to the Constitution. Recall that the Bill of Rights, or first 10 amendments to our Constitution ratified four years after the Constitution was signed. There are a variety of reasons for why the Bill of Rights was not initially included in the Constitution, as there was debate about it. However, one must keep in mind that prior to this time, it was unheard of for a government to share power with its people, but in this new system the People were finally made sovereign. If this was to be a government of, by and for the people, then a Bill of Rights would be necessary. It is also quite possible that the French Revolution which began with the storming of the Bastille in 1789 might have stimulated movement in this area. The thought of the French King Louie XVI, along with Marie Antoinette (of the "let them eat cake" fame) literally "losing their heads" via the guillotine likely made a strong impact on the first US Congress!

With this 4th element of power resting with the people themselves, the courts began dealing with issues involving balancing this new government power with these newly minted individual rights. Some government actions will invariably have a detrimental effect on the rights of some citizens. Often such infringements may not even be intended, but they nonetheless create disputes which must be resolved by the courts. In this regard, there are three so called "balancing tests" that the courts use to determine whether a Government restriction should stand or give way to a competing individual right.

The fundamental idea is that the Courts are actually "weighing" the rational justification of the government's restriction of individual rights. Simply stated, this implies that "Reasons have weight". Some of you may remember the hippie phrase of the 1970's.... "that's really *heavy*, man", meaning it had great significance (at least in the minds of those affected).[3]

The "WEIGHT" of "REASON"

In general, the greater the justification of the reason, the more likely it is that courts will uphold a governmental restriction. Since rational justification can vary according to the circumstances and the interests involved with each case, courts need a way to better quantify and communicate the significance of the justification. For this reason, terms of art are used to differentiate how "weighty" a particular justification is. Words like "rational", "substantial", and "compelling", are thus used to signify how much weigh should be given to the government argument.

Within the third Dimension of Constitutional Balance then, there are three separate balancing tests that the courts use for deciding these types of cases, especially with regard to 14th Amendment Due-Process or Equal protection cases:

1. The Rational-Basis Test: This is used to determine whether the Government entity is justified in restriction individual rights for health, safety, or welfare reasons. Examples might be State laws requiring seat belts, or motorcycle helmets. If a motorcyclist wanted to ride free, as I say "with the wind in his hair and bugs in his teeth", his liberty interest would have to give way to a rational justification that tips in favor of the State.

2. The Substantial Government Interest Test (Intermediate test) requires the Government entity to provide more justification that merely a rational basis. This test is generally applied to discrimination based on gender or legitimacy. An example would be a state law that prohibits an adopted child to be the executor of his or her deceased parent's estate. Here the State would have to show a "substantial" reason why this is needed.

3. The Compelling Interest Test (aka "Strict Scrutiny Test"). Here the Courts look "with a fine tooth comb" for a most compelling reason which an individual liberty should be restricted. This test applies to "fundamental rights" (listed or implied in the constitution/amendments). Again, the Patriot Act would be an example here.

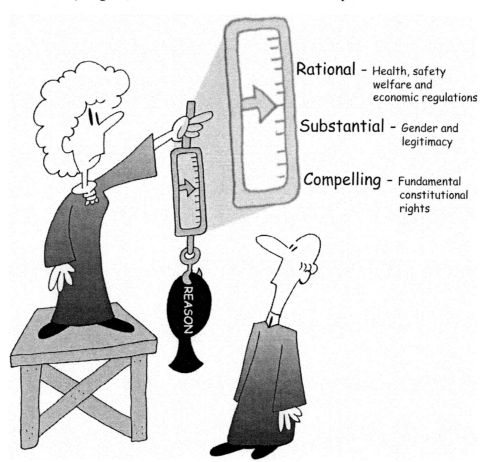

THE LANGUAGE OF RATIONAL JUSTIFICATION
BALANCING THE INTERESTS:

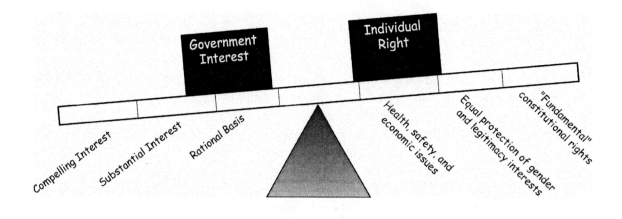

Compelling Interest · Substantial Interest · Rational Basis · Government Interest · Individual Right · Health, safety, and economic issues · Equal protection of gender and legitimacy interests · "Fundamental" constitutional rights

---

References:

1. http://en.wikipedia.org/wiki/John_Dalberg-Acton,_1st_Baron_Acton
2. Hartmann, Thom; Unequal Protection: The Rise of Corporate Dominance and Theft of Human Rights. Mythical research, Inc. 2002.
3. Recall from the Critical Thinking booklet that "significance" is an important term of art and is directly connected to the element of thought dealing with implications or consequences.

THE SCALES OF JUSTICE

Chapter 5: Basic Criminal Law Principles

Each one of the prior chapters has had a key word, which is the central theme for its content. Likewise, this chapter also has a key work, and that word is **protection**. Society needs to be protected from harms that may befall individuals or an individual's property, tangible, or otherwise. In the Constitutional Chapter, we have read about the evils of segregation in the Brown v. Board of Education case and in the films we have viewed. However, segregation does have its place in a civilized society. That is, the segregation of criminals from the mainstream of society! If a person is provided due process and has been found guilty **"beyond a reasonable doubt"** by a jury of his or her peers, then we deem it justifiable that such person (now a criminal) should be denied many of their otherwise inherent rights, and be segregated from the rest of society. We do this for various reasons that will be stated below.

Before we reach that point, however, we must discuss the basis of what it means to be designated a criminal. If society needs to be protected from "them", then society needs to have a mechanism by which it can properly decide who falls into that category of criminal. For purposes of clarification, an analogy is in order.

As I may have stated in class, "Law is like Chemistry". In fact, law is the chemistry of the intangible world. In the realm of the natural world, we define substances by the elementary molecules that make up their chemical structure. For example, water is H2O, Ammonia is NH4, Salt is NaCl, etc. Each of these substances is understood by the chemical composition of their elements. By the same token, legal concepts are also defined by their elementary nature. It will become increasingly important in this class to know and recognize the elementary structure of the various legal concepts we will be discussing, and how they might apply to the cases before us.

Let us begin then, with the most basic elementary structure of what we call **crimes.** The two most basic, or essential, elements of most all crimes are the mental element, "mens rea" (evil mind), and the action element, "actus rea" (evil act). In most cases, these two ingredients must be established by the State, via a **prosecutor,** beyond a reasonable doubt before a person can be **convicted** of a crime. Of course, one must recognize that one can have a guilty mind without committing an evil act. Fortunately for us, there are no thought police around to arrest those with such thoughts. Imagine how full the jails would be if it were otherwise! By the same token, one can also commit a bad act without an evil mind or intent. We have all seen the bumper sticker "……" happens (and often does), but it is only a crime (in most cases) if there was an evil intent which caused it. There are two varieties of situations where an evil act can be committed without an evil intent. The first is in the case of insanity, or diminished capacity. For example, a person might believe they are squeezing lemons, when in fact, they may be harming someone. In these situations, prison is not the solution for the individual involved. Society shows a degree of mercy for such poor souls by placing them in some form of mental institution in the hope that they might be treated for their illness. As we will learn, however, the so called "insanity defense" is quite difficult to establish and rarely succeeds. The second, and perhaps more interesting category of the lack of an evil mind is the person who knows what they are doing, but for some reason they do not believe it is wrong. Good examples of this situation is the person who shoots an abortion doctor, or burns a women's health clinic. From the criminal's perspective, they are not committing a crime, but trying to save the life of the unborn. An even more serious example would be that of so called suicide bombers who walk into crowed markets and then ignite a blast killing and maiming many. From their rather twisted mentality, they believe they have some higher calling beyond the laws of man. This, of course, is at the crux of what the West calls terrorism.

In any event, it is the interplay between evil intent and an evil act that make for good Hollywood screenplays. It is great drama to consider the tipping point between a mere wrongful thought and a full fledged criminal act. We will discuss some examples in class.

CRIME: A MATTER OF ELEMENTS

Having said the above, there is one situation that is the exception to the rule of requiring both the evil mind and evil act. That exception is referred to a "no fault" or "regulatory" crimes. That is, for these normally non violent crimes no mental fault is required. That is, the actus reus is sufficient in itself. For example, if one parks in a tow away zone, a police office will not inquire as to your state of mind. The fact that one parks improperly is sufficient to warrant the citation (a minor criminal act in most states). Other examples are selling adulterated food or products.

The Presumption of Innocence:

Recall that the laws for any given society are a reflection of it social, cultural, and political values. That being said, one of the most cherished values in the United States is that of freedom. Freedom not only in the physical sense, but also in the Intellectual sense. One of the gravest punishments one can have is to restrict that fundamental freedom. As a society, we value that freedom so much that, in a criminal case, we place the entire burden of proof on the State. If the State, through its prosecutor, can not find sufficient evidence to prove its case to a jury, then the charged person goes free. This is the so called presumption of innocence. A charged defendant need do nothing to prove his innocence, and indeed need not even take the witness stand due to his/her 5th Amendment Right against self incrimination. That is, a defendant need not be a witness against him or herself.

As a society, we are really saying that it is better for a guilty person to go free, than an innocent person go to jail. We also know that the legal system is not perfect, and does makes mistakes, virtually guaranteeing the above result. This is not to say that innocent people are not sometimes wrongly convicted, but on balance the system was designed to prevent it.[1] Needless to say, any man made system, such as the legal system has to be properly maintained and periodically revised in order to reasonably assure its effectiveness.

Degrees of Evilness or mental fault:

Given the above discussion of the essential elements of most crimes, a question may come to mind as to whether there are different states or degrees of evilness, or states of mind? We will see that there is such a distinction, and it is that distinction that is used as a basis for determining the level of punishment that a convicted criminal deserves. The worst mental state of evilness is the **"purposeful"** state of mind. This is a premeditated state by which the criminal has planned or otherwise thought about the evil act before they act itself. At common law, it was referred to a "malice aforethought". A person with this state of mind might be one who sets up an intricate plan to stalk and capture their victim(s). A person with this state of mind deserves the greatest punishment available by the legal system, which is not in conflict with Constitutional principles banning cruel and unusual punishment (8th Amendment).

The next most evil state of mind is said to be **"knowing"**. That is, the person committing a criminal act has not planned or thought about the act in advance, but they had knowledge of what they were doing at the time of the act itself. A common scenario is the so called crime of passion, where a cheating spouse, and perhaps his or her lover is knowingly harmed or killed in a fit of rage. Shortly following the event, the perpetrator feels great remorse, but it is too late as the crime has been committed. In a murder case, this might qualify for 2nd degree homicide.

Reckless behavior is the next most culpable state of mind. The hallmark of this mindset is total disregard for the welfare of others. The perpetrator is consumed with meeting their own needs despite the risk of harm that could be inflicted on others. Examples would be reckless driving by excessive speeding and weaving in and out of traffic lanes. If someone were to be killed in such an act, in most states a death could be attributable to the crime of **manslaughter.**

The above three categories of state of mind are said to be **subjective** in nature, and rest on the premise that it is reasonable to infer one's state of mind by the actions they engage in. In fact, that is what a jury is doing when it deliberates upon the evidence presented in a particular case. Such inferences will be upheld by the courts as long as all other factors of jury selection and deliberation are legally sufficient.

In contrast to the above three states of mind, the fourth of mental fault is said to be an **objective** rather than a subjective inquiry. By this it is meant that a fact finder, typically a jury) must gauge the accused state of mind by comparing his or her behavior to that of a

reasonable person in the same or similar circumstance. The concept of the so called reasonable person is in fact a fictitious entity largely borrowed from the area of **tort law**. This state of mind is referred to as **Negligent**. One is considered negligent if a jury finds, based upon the evidence presented, that a person failed to achieve that standard of behavior that a reasonable person would have achieved in similar circumstances. An example might be a person who suffers from epilepsy, but fails to take medication prior to driving a car on a long trip. A person should know that failing to take medication could cause a risk of having a seizure while driving. If a seizure were to occur in such circumstances, the perpetrator would likely be considered negligent in failing to take such medication before driving. If a death resulted therefrom, the charge would be **Negligent homicide.**

PURPOSEFUL

KNOWING   RECKLESS BEHAVIOR

NEGLIGENT

Having said all of the above, in certain situations the mental state of an accused criminal is totally irrelevant to the charge. There are, in fact, some crimes that require no mental intent whatsoever. Stated another way, these are crimes that require the 'actus reus" or evil act alone. These are referred to as "**mala prohibita**" crimes. They are wrong only because they are prohibited, not because they are "**mala in se**" or wrong in themselves, like the first four categories. Examples here would be parking in a tow away zone, tampering with food products; or, in some states, writing a bad check. These crimes may also be referred to as "**regulatory**" or "**no fault**" crimes, and are typically minor in comparison to the "male in se" category.

MALA PROHIBITA

LEVELS OF EVIL
THE DEGREE OF PUNISHMENT SHOULD FIT THE CRIME

How does Criminal punishment protect Society?

If we are to be protected by criminal laws, then any punishment or sanction meted out to a convicted criminal should reasonably achieve some protective purpose. What, then, are the possible protective functions of punishment? There are four classic purposes that justify the segregation and punishment of individuals convicted to committing crimes.

1. Specific Deterrence: Placing a convicted criminal in prison obviously prevents them from committing future crimes because it isolates the individual from society. However, that may also send a signal to others contemplating similar behavior.

2. General Deterrence: Is the signal sent to the general public that committing crimes can be costly in terms of time in prison, affect on one's reputation and employment potential. The loss of freedom to do what one pleases, as well as the discomforts and hazards associated with imprisonment also send a negative signal to others. These signals are though to deter persons on the margins from committing similar crimes.

3. Retribution: This is a psychological factor primarily affecting the friends and or family of a criminal's victim, but also the general feeling in society that one deserves the "just deserts" of their bad acts. The Old Testament admonishes us that "any eye for an eye, and a tooth for a tooth"[1] is justified in the pursuit of psycho-emotional closure. Psychologists sometimes refer to this as a "cathartic effect". It just makes us feel better knowing that a person committing a criminal act should suffer similar treatment as the victim. In other words, as "one sows, so shall they reap"[2]. Obviously, there is a strong moral, ethical or religious perspective at play here.

4. Rehabilitation: This is the most controversial purpose of criminal sanctions. Statititics show that only about a third of criminal are rehabilitated and do not return to prison.[3]

This is particularly the case with juvenile offenders.[4] It appears that an important determining factor is the age of the offender. The older a person is, the greater the chance that they can be rehabilitated back into society.

References:

1. **Stevens, Christina. "Subverting the Truth: A Structural Perspective on Wrongful Convictions"** *Paper presented at the annual meeting of the MPSA Annual National Conference, Palmer House Hotel, Hilton, Chicago, IL*, Apr 03, 2008 *Online <PDF>*. 2009-06-17 <http://www.allacademic.com/meta/p266022_index.html>

2. The phrase "**an eye for an eye**", Hebrew: עין תחת עין‎, *ayin tahat ayin*, is a quotation from Exodus 21:23–27 in which a person who has taken the eye of another in a fight is instructed to give his own eye in compensation. At the root of the non-Biblical form of this principle is that one of the purposes of the law is to provide equitable retaliation for an offended party. It defined and restricted the extent of retaliation in the laws of the Old Testament

3. The Old Testament stated it this way: they that plow iniquity, and sow wickedness, reap the same. (Job 4:8). At least 50 years before the birth of Christ, the Roman statesman, philosopher, and orator, Marcus T. Cicero, said, As you have sown so shall you reap. And in the New Testament we find, whatsoever a man soweth, that shall he also reap. (Galatians 6:7)

4. There are statistics showing that only 35 percent of inmates do not make their way back to prison upon their release. This leaves us with a large percentage of released criminals who do commit crimes and end up being repeat offenders. This poses a major difficulty to society as well as a strain. The government has to fork out huge sums to keep tabs on these possible repeat offenders as well as maintaining the prison systems. Needless to say, the possibility of releasing prisoners who might be repeat offenders is a threat to social safety. http://ezinearticles.com/?expert=Moses_Wright

5. Careful studies of criminal rehabilitation continue to find little payoff. Peter Greenwood and Susan Turner of RAND, for example, studied an experimental program that delivered significantly more than the usual treatment services to juvenile delinquents. The controlled experiment showed in a one-year follow up that (1) increasing supervision of offenders did not reduce recidivism and (2) there was no significant difference in the arrests or self-reported criminal activities of the experimental and the conventionally treated groups. *Peter W. Greenwood and Susan Turner, "Evaluation of the Paint Creek Youth Center: A Residential Program for Serious Delinquents," Criminology 31, May 1993, pp. 263-79; and Joan Petersilia and Susan Turner in Evaluating Intensive Supervision in Probation/Parole: Results of a Nationwide Experiment, May 1993, National Institute of Justice.*

Chapter 6:
Tort Law: Intentional

Our civil legal system provides an avenue for one who is injured or suffers damage which is caused by another person or business entity to collect a reasonable value for the effects that such injury has caused. The key word, therefore, for the Torts chapter is "compensation". Think of the tort system as a mechanism for establishing the reasonable market value for a whole host of possible harms. As opposed to a system of worker's compensation, where a 'scheduled benefit' dictates an amount of potential damages, the tort system provides for a more 'customized' approach. In this respect, a jury typically determines a damage award based upon the unique specifics of each individual case.

In effect, we are all responsible for the consequences that our actions may have on others around us, or those that may have other dealings with us. If harm befalls another person due to our actions, or inactions, then we would have the distinction be being legally referred to as a "tortfeasor" (one who commits a tort). Do not confuse a tortfeasor with a criminal. Recall that while crimes are committed against society as a whole, torts are typically committed against individuals within a community. Despite these fundamental differences, one act can be both a crime and a tort. A classic example would be the OJ Simpson case of the late 90's. While Mr. Simpson was acquitted on murder charges, he was found liable for the tort of "wrongful death" and ordered to pay compensatory damages. Of course, this was due to the different burden of proof standards for crimes (beyond a reasonable doubt) compared to the burden in a tort case (a preponderance of the evidence, or "more likely than not"). Also keep in mind that not all bad happenings are torts. There are still many, many unfortunate events that occur where no one is really to blame for injuries or damages. It is only where causation is established for a specific kind of tort, that a tortfeasor would be compelled to compensate the victim for their loss. In this way, a victim is said to be made whole, or otherwise compensated, by the tortfeasor through the tort system. This is usually achieved through monetary awards. The amount of compensation that can be quantified is referred to as **special compensatory damages**. This type of damage might include, but is not limited to, medical bills, lost wages, disability payments, as well as future medical bills and/or wage loss. **General compensatory damages** are for more intangible losses such as pain, disfigurement, and suffering. Some states might also award punitive damages on occasional for serious or reckless wrongdoing. Most states, including Washington, limit civil **punitive** damages to fraud cases or where there is statutory authority to award excess damages. There is much variability among state laws in the tort area, so it is somewhat difficult to generalize. However, there are typical majority and minority views or rules on a variety of tort topics among the states.

As was the case with crimes, the "law is like chemistry". Our ability to understand and appreciate the nature of torts is to know them by their elementary nature. The two broad classes of torts are 'intentional" and "unintentional" or negligence torts. Intentional in the tort context is not quite the same as intentional in the criminal context. There is no mens rea requirement for torts. One only need to intend the natural consequences of their actions. That is to say, they intend to complete a particular act, but not necessarily its consequences.

Specific Torts: Affecting person:

1. Assault: Intentionally placing another in fear or apprehension of imminent harm. Example: Pointing a knife at someone in a threatening manner. The apprehension or fear but be perceived as imminent and reasonable. For example, pointing a dripping water pistol at someone would likely not place them in reasonable fear of immediate harm.

2. Battery: Harmful or offensive contact: Example: Having the wrong organ removed during a surgery. Though assault and battery often go together, this example also points out that one may have an assault without battery, or vice versa. Also keep in mind that Assault and Battery could also rise to the level of criminal acts for which the perpetrator could end up in prison. Remember, however, that the tort system is concerned with compensating the victims for injuries arising out of such acts, while the criminal system is concerned with protecting society. That is, the same act could be both a crime and a tort. As you will recall from the previous chapter, however, the burden of proving a crime is much great than that required for a tort.

3. False Imprisonment: The unjust or unreasonable restraint of a person's freedom of movement. By unreasonable here we mean that there is no legitimate basis or reason for such restraint. This can take various forms including physical restraints, psychological restraints, and/or pharmacologic restraints through use of medications or drugs. The clearest examples are typically found among the very young, or elderly, as these are the most vulnerable victims. For example a patient is a nursing home may be restrained to their bed for no legitimate purpose thus causing injury. Interesting examples also appear in the news from time to time, as occurred in the Jet Blue case on Valentine's day of 2007.[*]

"FALSE" IMPRISONMENT?

Specific Torts: Affecting Reputation:

Tort law protects our ability to establish and maintain positive regard within our communities. Our reputation is how others see or talk about us. For example, when one says "John is reputed to be a good business person", it means that John has a positive reputation for business. Such regard can be difficult to achieve and usually requires a good deal of time and effort. It can be so important that it can even enhance the intangible value of such business. For example, in the sale of a business with a good reputation, it is common that a value be placed on the "goodwill" or positive reputation that the business has had, which will continue to attract loyal customers. A counter example might be a sign on a business stating "under new management" in an attempt to disassociate from the "badwill" of a prior owner!

The point is that reputation is something that a value can be placed upon. People can spend many years building up their reputations (think of credit scores). When someone unjustly taints or otherwise undermines one's hard earned reputation, that is a cause for individual and societal concern sufficient to warrant a tort action. The torts affecting such matters are as follows:

1. Defamation: Literally translated this means to take away someone's "fame", or to "de-fame" them. This torts comes in 2 main varieties:
   A. Slander- defaming through the spoken word, and/or
   B. Libel- defaming through writing or broadcast media, which might include radio, Television, or internet broadcasts.

2. Disparagement: This is analogous to defamation but is aimed at someone's products or services. For example, false claims that a certain fast food establishment sells tainted hamburgers, or that a particular service provider routinely gouges its customers.

In either case above, the specific <u>elements</u> of the defamatory conduct are:

a) That the statement made must be false (i.e. truth is always a defense),
b) Publically communicated (even a 3rd party is sufficient), and depending on whether the defamed person is a "public figure",
c) Malice (ill will) may be required. A public figure is essentially one who is in the public spotlight and capable of defending his or her reputation in the media. There are several privileged situations which would allow a defamatory statement to be made without legal recourse, but those will not be dealt with in this chapter.

Specific Torts: Affecting Emotions:

Historically, in order to prevail in a tort claim for damages, the plaintiff had the burden of proving the matter asserted by a preponderance of the evidence. As society recognized the importance of healthy emotions to total well being, it began to protect such interests against tortfeasors who might cause them harm. Strategically, however, it was very difficult to prove damage to something that could not be seen, or adequately measured. Emotional damage, if sought at all, must have been linked to a physical manifestation or harm before the courts would recognize an emotional component sufficient enough to warrant some measure of compensation. In other words, a gaping wound or obviously broken bone would provide a reasonable basis for warranting a remedy for the emotions.

Things changed significantly in the late 1960's and early 70's. For example, in the Massachusetts case of Agis v. Howard Johnson[1] in 1976. In this case, a waitress of the restaurant sued the owner and the manager of the restaurant alleging that the manager held a meeting with the waitresses at which he said that someone was stealing from the restaurant and until the identity of that person could be established he would begin firing all the waitresses in alphabetical order, that the manager then summarily dismissed the plaintiff solely because her name began with the letter "A," that, as a result of this act the plaintiff sustained emotional distress, mental anguish, and loss of wages, that the defendants' acts were reckless, extreme, outrageous, and intended to cause emotional distress and anguish, and that the defendants knew or should have known that their acts would cause such distress. The Court here decided that the conduct of the defendants was sufficiently "extreme and outrageous", and "beyond the bounds of human decency" as to justify compensation for the emotional injury. This became the standard pleading requirement for the tort of Intentional Infliction of Emotional Distress.

Much more controversial, and less accepted is the tort of negligent Infliction of Emotional Distress. Because it appears to have no definable limits and the potential claims that can be made under the theory are many, it is difficult to define what situations would give rise to such a claim. Due to this substantial uncertainty, most legal theorists find the theory to be unworkable. The case of Boyles v. Kerr, 855 S.W.2d 593 (Tex. 1993) is illustrative. In this case, the defendant secretly videotaped himself engaging in sexual activities with the plaintiff. The defendant then showed this videotape to numerous individuals and caused severe distress to the plaintiff. The plaintiff brought suit against the defendant, asserting a claim for negligent infliction of emotional distress. On appeal, the Texas Supreme Court observed that the facts did not support a claim of negligence. Rather, the Court noted, the facts clearly supported a claim of an intentional injury by the defendant and it was evident that the claim had been cast as "negligence" solely to obtain insurance coverage. The Court then went on to hold that Texas did not recognize a claim for negligent infliction of emotional distress and remanded the case to the trial court for consideration of a claim for intentional infliction of emotional distress.

Nonetheless, on occasion some state courts have upheld a 3rd party derivative claim in situations where someone may witness a family member enduring some traumatic experience.[3]

Specific Torts: Affecting Privacy Interests:

The right of privacy, or even the word "privacy" is not to be found in the Constitution, yet the U.S. Supreme Court has ruled that privacy is a right which is inherently implied by the 1st, 4th, 5th, and primarily the 9th Amendments to the U.S. Constitution. Griswold v.

Connecticut, 381 U.S. 479 (1965).[2] The 9th Amendment is particularly interesting in that it clearly leaves the door open to progressive judicial interpretation over time, stating: *"The enumeration in the Constitution, of certain rights, shall not be construed to deny or disparage others retained by the people"*. What this essentially means is that just because certain rights are not mentioned in the Constitution does not mean that they do not exist. Courts may not infer from other amendments or circumstances that an unlisted right may be unavailable to protect individuals from the government. This amendment is, in essence, a wonderful expression of intellectual humility! The kind referenced in the Paul-Elder critical thinking handbook we have used in class.[3] The consequence of this license for broad interpretation has resulted in a range of protections for privacy interests in the tort context. Thus, there are four torts that specifically affect that right:[4]

1. Appropriation (of name or likeness): Our legal system protects an array of property interests ranging from tangible forms of property such as real estate, automobiles, clothing, appliances, etc. To intangible forms such as contract rights, intellectual property, or entitlements. Thus courts have held that our own names and likenesses are a part of the intangible property rights we each own in our identity. Thus if someone takes control or ownership of such interest at our detriment, a tort cause of action may ensue. See White v. Samsung Electronics, 971 F. 2d 1395 (9th Cir. 1992).

2. Intentional Intrusion on Seclusion: Sometimes people living in cities will purchase telescopes, ostensibly to gaze upon the stars, but perhaps periodically to peek into a neighbor's house. Again, if injury of damage were to result, the tort of Intrusion might be argued. Keep in mind that there must be an expectation of privacy in the situation before a tort can be committed. For example, taking a photo of a person sleeping in a public part would not be sufficiently private to constitute a tortious act.

3. Public Disclosure of Private Facts: Somewhat similar to the situation above, is the tort of public disclosure. Each of us probably have some information that we dearly hold private, the disclosure of which could result in various sort of harm, including emotional and financial. For example, a health care worker may become aware of delicate private information about a public figure that might be embarrassing or costly if disclosed. If the health worker were to disclose the information without permission, then a tort situation could arise, if harm results from the disclosed information.

4. False Light: With the advent of computer and graphic technology, it has become increasingly possible to create false or distorted images of persons. If such an image were to place someone in a negative context which resulted in financial or emotional damages, such person could potentially recover the value of that loss from the tortfeasor under the theory of "false light".[5]

<u>Specific Torts: Affecting Property Interests:</u>

Historically, there are 3 major categories of property interests that tort law affects.

Real Property: Considered to be the land and anything that is appurtenant, or attached, to it. In other words, "real estate". In many states the attachments are also known as "fixtures". Torts affecting this interest is two fold:

1. Trespass: Going onto to someone elses' land, or leaving upon it something the owner does not wish there without permission.

2. Nuisance: This tort springs from the common law right of "quiet enjoyment". That is, an owner of property also has acquired the intangible right to enjoy the property peacefully, and without unreasonable interference from obnoxious or annoying actions of neighboring property owners.

Personal Property: This is tangible movable property, excepting financial instruments and related documents. Tortious interference of such property interests includes:

1. Trespass: Similar to trespass to real property, and unwanted and destructive action to one's personal property gives rise to this tort. For example, a person could mark up a student's book without that person's permission, thereby damaging the value of the book for resale.

2. Conversion: This is defined as taking "dominion and control" of another's property in a manner inconsistent with the expectations of the true owner. A person borrowing a car to go to the store, but then driving it around town for several hours might be an example. This could also be the sweater that you loaned to a fried which you never got back. Also the purchase or possession of a stolen car could be conversion, even if the purchaser did not know it was stolen.

Intangible Property: As opposed to tangible forms of property, this is property that can not be touched or even seen, Yet, our legal system provides property rights in such things. There are three main categories of this type of property; intellectual property (the ownership of ideas), contract rights (ownership of promised obligations), and entitlements such as medicare benefits, unemployment insurance, food stamps, etc. The torts that affect these rights are:

1. Interference with Contractual relations: If two parties are already bound by contract, then it would be improper for someone to interfere to undermine the obligations between the parties. For example, if George Steinbrener of the New York Yankees somehow enticed Ichiro Susuki to leave the Seattle Mariners and play for more money in New York, Mr. Stenbrener would face an interference with contract claim by the Seattle Mariners. In essence, think of this tort as a form of trespass to intangible property.

2. Patent, Copyright, or Trademark infringement: If a person were to steal another's idea for a product, service, or adverting methods, this would be a tortuous attack on such intangible rights of the patent, copyright or trademark holder. For electronic and audio-visual media, unauthorized reproduction and distribution is referred to as **piracy.**

3. Fraudulent misrepresentation in attainment of property or entitlements. Making false claims for various government benefits would fall into this category. For example, providing false identification to become eligible for some benefits is a common concern of governmental agencies. The abuse of a charitable status has also been a problem, in that victims may often be reluctant to make any legal claims due to feelings of embarrassment which might result in making their situation public. See Patterns of Abuse at United Way: http://www.nytimes.com/1992/04/04/us/united-way-finds-pattern-of-abuse-by-former-chief.html

4. Identity theft: As stated in the prior chapter, this form of "white collar" crime can also be the basis for a civil tort if the victim seeks compensation for harm or damages suffered at the hands of such tortfeasor. Unfortunately, for many victims, the tortfeasor/criminal may not have much in the way of assets to compensate the lowly victim.

References:

1. Debra Agis v. Howard Johnson, Inc. 371 Mass. 140, 1976
   Note: In the 1968 landmark decision of _Dillon v. Legg_, 68 Cal. 2d 728 (1968) the Supreme Court of California was the first court to allow recovery for emotional distress alone – even in the absence of any physical injury to the plaintiff – in the particular situation where the plaintiff simply witnessed the death of a close relative at a distance, and was not within the "zone of danger" where the relative was killed.
2. Griswold v. Connecticut, 381 U.S. 479 (1965), was a landmark case in which the Supreme Court of the United States ruled that the Constitution protected a right to privacy. The case involved a **Connecticut** law that prohibited the use of contraceptives. By a vote of 7-2, the Supreme Court invalidated the law on the grounds that it violated the "right to marital privacy".
3. Richard Paul and Linda Elder: Miniature Guide to Critical Thinking.
4. Restatement (Second) of Torts §652D provides:

   One who gives publicity to a matter concerning the private life of another is subject to liability to the other for invasion of his privacy, if the matter publicized is of a kind that

(a) would be highly offensive to a reasonable person, and

(b) is not of legitimate concern to the public.

Unlike defamation, there is no requirement that the publicized information be false.[1] The tort of publication of private facts "involves the publication of true but intimate or private facts about the plaintiff, such as matters concerning the plaintiff's sexual life or health."[2]

5. In *Peoples Bank & Trust Co. v. Globe Int'l, Inc.* 786 F. Supp. 791, 792 (D. Ark. 1992), a tabloid newspaper printed the picture of a 96-year-old Arkansas woman next to the headline "SPECIAL DELIVERY: World's oldest newspaper carrier, 101, quits because she's pregnant! I guess walking all those miles kept me young." The woman (not in fact pregnant), Nellie Mitchell, who had run a small newsstand on the town square since 1963, prevailed at trial under a theory of false light invasion of privacy, and was awarded damages of $1.5M. The tabloid appealed, generally disputing the offensiveness and falsity of the photograph, arguing that Mitchell had not actually been injured, and claiming that Mitchell had failed to prove that any employee of the tabloid knew or had reason to know that its readers would conclude that the story about the pregnant carrier related to the photograph printed alongside. The court of appeals rejected all the tabloid's arguments, holding that "[i]t may be . . . that Mrs. Mitchell does not show a great deal of obvious injury, but . . . Nellie Mitchell's experience could be likened to that of a person who had been dragged slowly through a pile of untreated sewage . . . [and] few would doubt that substantial damage had been inflicted by the one doing the dragging."

Chapter 7:
Tort Law: Negligence and Strict Liability

In addition to Intentional Torts, there are also times when unintentional acts can result in legal liability. These types of acts need not be intended at all in the criminal or intentional tort context, but are based upon failures to abide be certain **Duties of Care**. The neglect of a legal duty owed is termed **"Negligence"**; and in keeping with the "law is elementary" principle, is based upon the existence of all of the following components:

1. A Duty Owed (Standard of Care)
2. Breach of such duty
3. Causation ("In fact", as well as foreseeability). Together, these are often referred to as "Proximate cause".
4. Damage or Injury

If any of the above elements are missing, then the injury is simply an unfortunate event or accident, and no liability attaches.

Duty:

Where do duties come from? They can arise in a variety of ways including, but not limited to, job descriptions, employee manuals, standards of practice for various professions, policy and procedure manuals and the like. In addition, we can even impose duties upon ourselves. For example, we have no duty to help strangers or pick up hitchhikers. However, should we ever choose to assist in this manner, there would be a self-imposed duty not to leave the person in a worse position that we found them. Special relationships may also call for special duties. For example, common carriers and innkeepers are subject to a greater duty of care to their guests because of their relationship and the control that they have over the public's surroundings. Similarly, family or caretaker relationships are often subject to a greater degree of duty as well.

Breach of Duty:

Once a legal duty is established, then one may be bound not to allow their behavior to fall below such standard. Keep in mind that the establishment of a legal duty, does not necessarily imply that the duty has been breached. However, if there is evidence that a duty has been breached, then a further inquiry into causation occurs.

Causation:

With regard to this element, there are two distinct forms of cause.

A. Cause in Fact ("But for" causation): Provides that there is a direct link between the breached duty and any injury or damage that may have resulted. For example, an inattentive driver talking on a cell phone who strikes a person in a crosswalk was be the "but for", or cause in fact of the pedestrian's injuries.

B. Foreseeability: Give the above, this does not necessarily mean that liability will attach if the victim or the accident was not reasonably foreseeable. In the example above, if the injury party is struck and killed by lightening while laying in the crosswalk, it would be too tenuous to make the driver liable for the pedestrian's death. See the classic case of <u>Palsgraph v. Long Island Railway.</u>[1]

In other words, while cause in fact might establish causation between the breached duty and the resulting injury, the foreseeability factor limits how far liability will extend. I like to think of the "rock in the pond" analogy. The rock will cause a "ripple effect" out from where the rock strikes the water, but it is hardly likely that a small boat 50 yards from the splash would capsize due to its effect. It is simply a very remote and unforeseeable consequence! As the court in the <u>Palsgraph</u> case put it, one must be in the so called "zone of danger" before liability exposure occurs. When cause in fact and foreseeability are united in this way, it is most commonly referred to as **Proximate cause.**

Superseding Cause:

Because we are all creatures of time, one must also consider the possibility of intervening forces occurring between an alleged cause and its arguable effect. There is always the possibility that something else could happen which might break the chain of causation. If the intervening event is so significant that it would no longer be reasonable to claim that cause "A" resulted in effect "B", then that intervening force is referred to as **superseding** and becomes the major cause of such effect. For example, if an automobile strike a pedestrian at night, the fact that night is a normal daily occurrence is an intervening, but not superseding, force and does not relieve the driver of liability. On the other hand, if someone pushed the pedestrian in front of the car, the one pushing the victim becomes the superseding cause of any injury sustained by the victim. This would thereby relieve the defendant driver from all or partial liability for the harm done. Keep in mind, however, that in comparative negligence states a jury (if instructed) could still apportion liability between co-defendants.

Joint Causes:

Sometimes two or more factors combine to cause a tortuous result. In some of these instances, it may be difficult or impossible to determine which of the factors were the actual cause of the damage. In such circumstances, a court could instruct the jury that if they find that either factor could have caused the effective injury, then they could both be liable as **substantial factors** in the outcome. In this instance, each contributing defendant would be considered jointly and severally liable in proportion to an ultimately contribution determined by the "trier of fact" (jury in most cases). In the purest form of **joint and several liability,** an injured plaintiff could recover damages their entire damages from any of the defendants. Consequently, if one defendant could not pay, then another joint defendant might have to bear the entire burden. Because of the potential for harsh results, especially when States are named defendants, most state legislatures have severely limited or abolished this effect of joint liability in situations where the plaintiff is partially at fault for their own injury (i.e. contributorily negligent).

Injury or Damage:

In keeping with the basic purpose of tort claims, that is, to provide a system of compensation for injured or damaged victims, there must be some measurable damage for which to compensate. In other words, one could breach an existing duty, but cause on very minor damage or no damages at all. Therefore, there would be nothing to compensate for. An area of controversy emerged in the late 1960's with regard to emotional damages. Prior to this time, one could not recover for emotional distress, even if intentional, unless there was also a physical manifestation of the injury. Consequently, it would be easy to conclude that a person was in emotional distress if there were "bleeding from the ears" in some injury. This all changed in several cases in the 1960's and 70's, where courts began to hold that damages for emotional distress could be obtained in situations where the defendant's conduct was "extreme and outrageous", or "beyond the bounds of human dignity".[2]

Forms of Negligence:

There are 3 distinctive forms of Negligence that can have a significant effect on whether a particular negligence case is proven by a preponderance of the evidence.

A. Common Law Negligence: This is the typical type of negligence described above. Each of the elements of this concept must be established in order for a plaintiff to prevail in a claim for damages.

B. Negligence "Per Se": This type of negligence involves the breach of a statute, ordinance, county code or other regulation. If the statute, ordinance, code or regulation is intended to protect a specific class of persons or entities, and the statute is not complied with, then duty and breach are presumed. This means that the plaintiff need only establish the causation and damage by a preponderance of the evidence in order to recover for their documented injuries.

C. Res Ipsa Loquitor (The Act speaks for itself): Some damages usually do not happen in the absence of Negligence. The common law has adapted to these situations by shifting the burden of proof to the alleged defendant. Requirements for evoking this doctrine is as follows:

   a. The act normally doesn't happen in the absence of negligence

   b. The defendant maintains exclusive control of the instrumentality of harm (e.g airplane, railroad, chemical plant, etc)

   c. The defendant has greater access to evidence.

In an airplane crash case, for example, statistic show that most crashes are due to pilot error or maintenance issues, certainly the passengers have no control over the aircraft, and the airline is much better able to produce evidence of flight history, maintenance records, pilot data than would be a victim of family thereof.

In order to difficulty in prevailing in a negligence claim, therefore, it it strategically easier to prevail in a Res Ipsa Loquitor case, than either Negligence Per Se or Common Law Negligence case. Because of the shifting of the burden of proof, it the defendant is unable to produce evidence of the absence of liability, the defendant then loses the case.

In a Negligence "per se" case, the plaintiff need only prove causation and damages, while in the Common Law negligence case, the plaintiff must prove all four of the elements of negligence on a "more likely that not" (preponderance) basis.

Duties of Possessors of Land:

In keeping with the general theme of duties, the possessor of land or real estate owns a duty of care to those that may enter upon it. This duty applies to owners as well as renters, but the duties of renters are often limited only to the living area of their residence. As we have learned previously, the best answer to any legal question is that "it depends" on the circumstances. In this case the dependent variable of duty of care, depends on the independent variable of the legal classification of persons. That is, the duty of care depends upon the classification or category of persons entering the premises. Fortunately, there are only three possible categories in the common law legal systems:

1. Trespasser: Sometimes one wanders where one should not go, or don't have permission to be. Nonetheless, a minimal legal duty is owed even the trespasser. That is, one may not intentionally harm the trespasser for his/her transgressions. In other words, it would not be proper or legal to sick your guard dog on such an unfortunate individual.

TRESPASSERS   DUTY NOT TO INTENTIONALLY HARM

2. Licensee: Here we need recall that in the old common law sense, "to grant license" to someone was to grant permission. Thereby a licensee has received express or implied permission to enter upon the possessor's land for a particular purpose. The duty of the possessor in this case, would be to warn or remove dangers known by the possessor, but unknown to the licenses. The possessor discharges his or her duty by removing ice from the walkway, or warning of an uneven pathway, etc.

Hi Sally! Come on over for lunch, but *be careful.* There's a patch of ice on the walkway.

LICENSEE

3. Invitee: Sometimes this gets confused with the licensee status. For example, one might think that if you invited someone to dinner at your house, they would be an invitee. However, they would legally be considered a licensee because they were given tacit permission to enter the premises. The true legal invitee is either a (A) Business Visitor who is in the premises for a commercial purpose, or (B) is a Public invitee who is in a public park, campground, swimming pool, library, etc. The duty of care owed to the invitee is of the highest order. In addition to warning or removing known dangers, they must also be on the lookout for "potential" dangers to the public. In essence, this essentially boils down to the phrases of "Inspect, Discover, and Repair" known, as well as hidden or potential dangers to the public.

Customers will be showing up soon. I put some salt on the ice to melt it, but I better put a sign over it just to keep people safe.

ICE

INVITEE   **duty to inspect, discover and repair**

59

In analyzing premises liability cases, then, the courts must first determine the classification of the entering party before they can determine the level of duty owed them. It is also important to keep in mind that classifications may readily change, depending on what is taking place on the premises. For example, one be shopping in a large retail store with a child who needs to use the restroom. See that none is readily available, the person could ask a clerk or salesperson for permission to use the "employee's only" rest room. Upon permission being granted, the legal status of the person thus changes from invitee to that of licensee for the purpose of using the rest room. In a similar fashion, the status of the invitee would change to that of a trespasser if they used the employee's only rest room without proper permission. In the event of some accident and injury, (e.g. box falling on someone's head) a legal question would be raised as to the liability of the property owner. That question would be answered by first classifying the status of the person at the time and place of the accident, and then applying the proper duty of care rule for that situation.

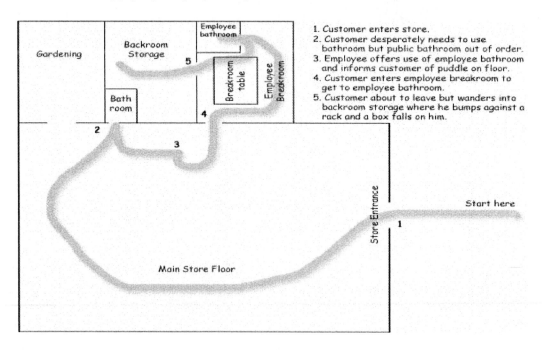

Defenses to Negligence:

Fortunately for the alleged tortfeasor, there are several legal defenses available. Note that these defenses are in addition to the defense that, with the exception of Res Ipsa Loquitor situations, the plaintiff fails to state a claim based on lack of one or more of the essential elements of Negligence. For example, a defendant can claim no duty, no breach of that duty, no causation ("but for" and/or proximate), or that no cognizable injury occurred. In addition, a defendant can also make a **counterclaim**, alleging that the plaintiff is liable to him/her for damages. Other defenses are as follows:

1. Contributory Negligence (the minority rule): There are only about 5 states left which provide a defendant this argument: if the plaintiff is at all responsible for their own.

2. Injury, they cannot recover anything from the defendant. This rather harsh rule is allowed only one exception termed the "last clear chance". In such exception, the defendant is only liable to a partially at fault plaintiff if they had a clear chance to avoid the injury, but didn't take it. For example, if a defendant sees a person jay walking several blocks away, they cannot avoid liability if they hit them because they had an opportunity to avoid the accident and didn't take it. On the other hand, if a jay walker were to dart out in front of them while driving, obviously the last clear chance exception would not apply.

3. Comparative Negligence: (the majority rule). Increasingly, the states have allowed juries to apportion liability between the plaintiff and defendant in the form of a **special verdict**.[3] There are two primary forms of this system, **pure and modified** versions. In the pure form, a plaintiff can recover damages regardless of their level of fault. For instance, in a $10,000 claim with the jury finding the plaintiff 90% responsible for their own injuries, the plaintiff could still recover 10%, or $1,000. In the modified form, however, a plaintiff can only recover if they are less than 50% responsible for their own injuries.[4]

4. Assumption of Risk; A defendant can claim that a plaintiff **knowingly and voluntarily** assumed a risk of injury by engaging in some specified activity. In other words, one can not assume a risk they do not know.

Some defendants have attempted to minimize their risk exposure by having a potential plantiff sign a **waiver or release of liability form.** However, almost all courts have ruled that any such attempt may not be overbroad and must be specifically tailored to the activity engaged in. It would thus be improper, as against public policy, to allow a defendant to absolve any and all liability for its actions. To allow such blanket waivers would only create a disincentive for some companies or individuals to take reasonable precaution for their actions.

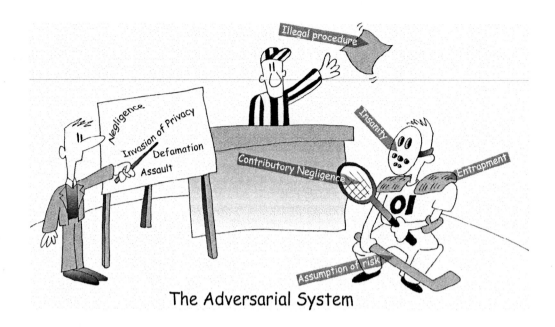

The Adversarial System

Strict Liability:

In contrast to the above, there are some forms of liability that are based upon the type of activities engaged in by a defendant. For these sorts of activities there are few, if any, defenses allowable. In other words, liability may attach to these activities even though great care may have been taken. Specific laws vary from state to state, however the fundamentals of strict liability remain fairly constant, and fall into three main categories:

1. Unreasonably dangerous activities (ultrahazardous acts): This set of activities would include things like working with explosives, toxic materials, radiation, mining, crop dusting and related acts.

2. Keeping of Animals: This is divided into two distinct areas, the keeping of wild animals versus domesticated animals. A domesticated animal is one which is kept for the benefit of humans. These could be pets like dogs and cats, or farm animals like cows, sheep, and goats. Lions, Tigers and Bears (oh my!) would be considered wild. Sometimes this becomes a question of fact for a jury to determine.

   In any event, keepers of wild animals are liable for any harm caused by their animal. Keepers of domestic animals, on the other hand, are generally only liable for harm caused by animals that are trespassing, or who they know are dangerous (the so called "one free bite" rule).

3. Products Liability: Persons or businesses who put products into the "stream of commerce" have a legal duty to make sure such products are safely made in

order to minimize harm to the ultimate consumer. This category is further subdivided into 3 main areas:

A. Design Defects: Although the products is properly made, its design may prove to be flawed and dangerous. The 3 wheeled all terrain vehicle (ATV) of the 1980's is a good example. The product proved to be inherently unstable and subject to roll over due to its design. The Ford Pinto case of the 1970's is another disastrous example.

B. Manufacturing Defects: It was once said that automobiles manufactured on a Monday or Friday were inherently less reliable than cars made on other days.

C. Failure to Warn: Most everyone has noticed the ubiquity of warning signs that abound in our society. Though some seem rather ridiculous (e.g. "do not use hairdryer in the shower"), they all serve at least two important legal purposes. That is, to manage or avoid the risk of legal liability while preventing needless injuries to the public. It is in this area that some states have allowed the defense of Assumption of Risk, as discussed above. Other states require product manufacturers and/or sellers to not only anticipate the normal uses of their products, but also to consider how the product may be misused and warn against those uses as well! Critics have argued that all of this regulation and liability exposure costs producers too much money and may even stifle the creativity for new products. Further, those costs are typically passed on to consumers who pay more for the product because of testing, safety features, and/or warnings. To those critics, one might respond with the old admonition: "An once of prevention is worth a pound of cure". That is, better to prevent injuries in the first place than to pay for them later in money and suffering.

In addition to compensating victims for injuries resulting from these acts, the tort system also creates a **deterrent** effect by making an example of defendants who become liable for the consequences of their actions. In so doing, other similarly situated defendants may take more care in order to avoid similar liability. A further deterrent is sometime warranted by the imposition of **punitive or exemplary** damages. Such damages extend beyond compensating the victim for the value of their injuries, in order to provide a more severe sanction for gross negligent behaviors. Some states have limited the extent to which punitive damages may be applied. For example, in Washington it is generally limited to fraudulent activities or by statutory scheme such as in the Consumer Protection Act (RCW 19.86).

References:

1. Palsgraph v. Long Island Railroad.
2. Agis v. Howard Johnson, Inc.
3. In the case of Washington State, the legislature repealed the old contributory negligence standard, and adopted a pure comparative fault system in 1973.
4. Note that the states vary in terms of the percentage of fault a plaintiff must have in order to prevent recovery. Some states have a 50% or more rule, while others require 49%. http://www.mwl-law.com/PracticeAreas/Contributory-Neglegence.asp

Appendix 1:

The Practical Logic of Critical Thinking: *As extrapolated from the Paul-Elder Model.*
F. Primiani, J.D.

As we proceed through this course, please keep in mind the process orientation of the course design. That is, the main purpose of this class is to improve your thinking skills, and thereby any work products that emanate therefrom. If you learn useful information about the subject matter in general that will be a bonus, but what really matters is whether you improve your ability to think, reason, communicate, and make good judgments.

Therefore, please keep in mind the general logic of critical thinking, as described below:

Typical Definition of Critical Thinking: The process of analyzing thought, evaluating thinking by use of defined and accepted intellectual standards, and reformulating thinking based upon the results of assessment. Objective self-reflection is a necessary prerequisite to Critical Thinking.

Purpose: To improve the quality of thought, which enables improved judgments and choices.

Question at Issue: How does one improve the quality of thought, and thereby of life?

Information: Any and all information which can be directly or indirectly perceived. Further information may be extracted and refined by relevant and focused questioning.

Assumptions: Thinking is a skill, which can be analyzed, practiced, and improved. It is a process that can be applied to any content or substance. It is a "system opening system". Further, critical thinking can influence emotions and behaviors. Knowledge that is "discovered" by a logically consistent internal process is more meaningful than information that is passively acquired. Unstructured and undisciplined thinking is inherently flawed. A self directed and reflective thinker is best suited for acquiring meaningful knowledge.

Concepts Used: Substance and process, inert information, activated knowledge, theory, reason, analysis, interpretation, inference, implication, analogy, relevance, accuracy, precision, clarity, depth, breadth, logic, significance, learning, teaching, education, ignorance, intelligence, intellectual standards and traits. Self actualization.

Inferences and Conclusions: Judgments are based upon a thoughtful analysis of the parts of thinking, and evaluated by agreed upon intellectual standards. Good thinkers routinely self analyze, question, and evaluate their thinking before drawing inferences and conclusions. A critical thinker does not "jump to conclusions"; rather they tend to reserve judgment until they are satisfied with such self analysis. On the other hand, a critical thinker's conclusions are generally viewed as being tentative. New information may always lead to altered conclusions.

Implications/Consequences: Improved judgments result in improved choices. Better choices lead to more self directed, and fulfilling lives. As the critical thinker further fosters, develops, and practices critical thinking, positive intellectual traits will more likely evolve. These are: Intellectual integrity, honesty, humility, empathy, autonomy, courage, perseverance, discipline, fairmindedness, and confidence in reason. These traits are of benefit to a civilized society.

Point of View: Critical Thinkers ultimately place their faith in reason, and the untapped potential of the human mind. At the same time, they recognize that not all knowledge is readily apparent. There is always more to be known and understood. In other words, there is more that is unknown than known. Life is an awe inspiring journey of continual exploration.

Appendix 2:

Meeting Standards in Case Presentations

Hopefully, you have read and understand the standard rubric which will be used to grade student case presentations. Here are some added examples of how one might use various techniques to achieve those standards. This is not intended to be an exhaustive list, but should give you a few ideas to think about as you prepare your presentations. Good luck and try to have fun!

Clarity:
*   Relationship Trees- to illustrate how the parties are related
*   Symbolic Illustrations
*   Definitions of relevant terms
*   Role play – opening activity
*   Example of clauses in contracts, or documents at issue
*   Use of highlight or bolding important terms

    Other ideas:
    A. Analogies (using a real world analogy to clarify some abstract concept)
    B. Simplification- finding a basic pattern in the conflict story that clears up a concept (Due process, promissory estoppel: promise, reliance, detriment, negligence, contract, etc.)
    C. Timelines (when lots of dates involved)
    D. Venn diagrams (e.g. Morality vs. Law)
    E. Maps or drawings of property
    F. Metaphors (shaking hands for contracts, dove for peace, etc.)

Depth:

Remember, this is "thinking outside the book"
*   Compare and contrast with other related cases.
*   Find full language of Laws, Rule, or other concepts
*   News, or journal articles related to your issues
*   "Law review" articles (provides a historical context). Can sometimes find online.
*   "Shepardizing" for status of current law. This means how the case was treated in future cases (precedent followed, distinguished, or rejected). This is a bit more technical, see me if questions.
*   Related personal experiences

Breadth:

        A. Plaintiff v. Defendant
        B. Secondary perspectives
- Economic
- Political
- Social
- Cultural
- Moral
- Philosophical
- Views from other classes you've taken

Significance:
* Consider other options the parties may have chosen
* How could similarly situated parties avoid problems like this in the future.
* What might happen if the court decided differently (comparative implications)
* Was the case cited in other appellate opinions? If so, to what effect?
* What consequences occurred because of your case?

Accuracy:
* All facts correctly stated in the conflict story
* The procedural court history is correct (which court found what)
* Correct identification of plaintiff, defendant, appellant, respondent, the judge, district court, rules of law, reasoning of the court, and the conclusion reached.

Precision:
* If several issues are raised, clearly and correctly stated main issue.
* State elements or factors to be considered:
  e.g. what are the Elements of various concepts as Offer, Negligence, Commercial Speech, Procedural Due Process, etc.

Here are some other strategies you can use for "finer detail":

        C. listing exceptions to legal rules. For example, the Statute of Frauds has a number of exceptions for each rule. Knowing these adds to a precise understanding of the principles.
        D. Stating the specific language of a statute or regulation involved in a case (eg. RCW 64 vs. RCW 63.10.010 b (2)).
        E. Stating a specific legal "test" that may emanate from a <u>precedent case</u> (e.g. the "minimum contacts test" for long arm jurisdiction, or the "Hudson test" for commercial free speech).

Note: A precedent case, can also be used as a <u>Concept</u>. That is, a Rule or Test may emanate from a case as a concept or idea that can be used for future disputes of a similar type. See above.

Relevance:

Relevance to the text: What does the case tell us about what's in the book?
Do the related cases sited have anything to do with the main case? Do they help us understand it better by comparing or contrasting to the related cases.

E.g, "This related case is an example of how summary judgment works", but here the court gave an opinion opposite from our main case because of these factual differences".....

Logic:
Correctly covered all elements of thought.

   A. no confusion between elements (that is, facts are not listed as implications, questions are not stated as conclusions, points of view are not listed as consequences, etc. Be aware of the language you are using to express your thinking about the presentation.
   B. inferences lead to conclusions
   C. conclusions lead to implications/consequences, etc.

Organization/efficiency:
No "drag" or overlap in presentation. It flowed smoothly and transitions well. Print on the PPT concise and clear – no redundancy, easy to read, etc. Transition between group members was smooth and does not repeat what a previous person said.

General Interest:
   • Engaging presentation in own words (avoid just reading some "cut and paste"quotes from the opinion in a very monotone voice). Summarize what the court is saying in your own words!.
   • Survey of students
   • Appealing charts/ppt
   • If your case deals with a company? Can you use their company website to add interest or detail?
   • Integrating Media like audio, video clips, sound effects, animations etc.

Note: Some Strategies that may relate to more than one standard (i.e. mixed standards). In this case, the instructor will use the "predominant thrust of factor" test (similar to goods vs. services cases) to determine which is more prominent. That is, double credit is unlikely to be given.

   Examples:

   A. Presenting a "dissenting" opinion in a case can add depth (if not in book), but it could also be viewed as another point of view, which could also add interest.

B. Adding media could be adding interest, and also depth or point of view
C. Stating a section of the Restatement of contracts or torts could be depth, but also precision, etc.
D. Referring to a related case could add depth, but could also be a concept (if a precedent case)

Further Important Note: Points will be given for use of <u>different</u> <u>strategies</u> for achieving a standard. That is, multiple use of examples, illustration, etc, will only count as ONE strategy for 1 point. Keep this in mind while developing your presentations.

Rev: 6/08 FP

Appendix 3:

Law Courses: Case Method Groups

Group Contract Assignment:

During the course of this quarter you will be learning about the role of Contracts in a stable business environment. We will discuss principles of formation, performance, and breach. As part of the holistic design of this course, each group will be responsible for negotiating a workable agreement (learning contract) with their respective team members. This will be a good "hands on" way to become familiar with how the world of contracts has applications to our everyday activities. As we proceed through the quarter, you will learn about elements, doctrines and clauses that you can use in your group situation. The purpose of this assignment will be to determine how well you can prevent or manage issues of conflict that may arise in your group activities.

Typical Examples of conflicts that tend to arise when 2 or more students attempt to work together on class projects might be the following:

   a. What mechanism will be used to decide who does what?
   b. Who will be responsible to assigning group work?
   c. What happens in the event of inadequate or incomplete contributions of a member?
   d. In addition to point reallocations, what remedies will be available for a member's non performance.
   e. What kind of guidelines will be used for group task planning
   f. What type of things should be in writing vs oral agreement
   g. What is the best way to allocate time and energy resources of the group.
   h. Which members have expertise in certain areas that the group may defer to?
   i. What constitutes substantial performance?

As each group proceeds with its tasks, each member should be on the lookout for potential disputes that can be addressed in a contract before the dispute arises, and think about contract language that might work in an agreement.

Method of Developing Contract Language:

Any member of the group may propose contract language to address a particular group issue. In order to do so, they will make an informal motion to their group members for inclusion of such language. At least one other member of the group must "second" the motion. Then the group should meet or communicate to discuss whether such language should be included in the Contract. A majority vote of the group will be necessary to add the language. In the event of a tie, then the group will either:

   1. negotiate their difference, or

   2. prepare an alternate version of the contract. However, no more than 2 contract versions will be allowed.

The group will turn in a draft on its contract midway through the quarter, and then again near the end of the quarter for a grade. The grade will be based upon the design, clarity, effectiveness, and creativity of the agreement. Below is a Template for the Group Performance Contract that can be used as a starting point for modifications.

Sample Template for Group Presentation Contract

Group Presentation Contract:

Introductory Language stating Group members, age or capacity, legality, consideration, mutual assent. Also that the team members are not being influenced by any invalidating factors. Below are some other clauses you may consider adding to your agreement.

Purpose:

The purpose of this agreement is to:

Team Organizational Structure:

The leadership structure for the group will be:

Mechanism for determining and achieving Division of Labor

Grade or Point allocation System

Logistical issues: Frequency of meetings, time/place manner issues

Notification Issues: For example, when should the presentation material be sent to the producer or editor, and it what form?

Definition and Remedies for Breach:

Process for Contract Modification (you may use a version of the process in "Method for Developing Contract Language" on the Assignment Page).

Whether there will be any Conditions, Incentive, or exclusion Clauses

"Compensation" Issues

For Example, will extra points be given for group leadership, editing, or creation of power points?, or will such tasks be rotated among the group members? If so, how?

Whether the Contract will be "Integrated" or not?

Determining Rules or Choice of Law to interpret Contract

Appendix 4:

Case Method Presentations: Preparatory Activities for Significance

Signs are everywhere around us. Pointing out destinations, labeling buildings, warning us of dangers, and otherwise helping us understand our surroundings. They point out what is, what was, or what is likely to happen in our environment.

The facts that signs may be there, however, does not necessarily mean that they will be read or understood. How many times have we all "pulled" a door when the sign said "push", or vice versa? Also, people may different perceptions about what is significant.

Given the disparity of perception or appreciation among individuals, it is often necessary that a common idea of significance be communicated and understood among and between persons who may be affected such important event. For example, to the trained eye, certain weather patterns may give rise to concerns about public safety that must be transmitted in a manner that is both clear and likely to be perceived as important. In the Paul-Elder model, the standard of significance is keenly tied to the thinking elements of implications and consequences. The distinction being that while implications are likely to happen in the future, consequences have already happened. Both are significant, but one looks forward, and the other back in time.

The following drill will assist you in appreciating and explaining significance to others.

<u>Significance Exercise:</u>

1. Work in groups of 3 or 4
2. Each person will think of a concept, fact, theory, or issue of great consequence or significance in any course which the student may be familiar. You may choose something that you are very comfortable in explaining, or if you are adventurous, something less assuring.
3. Write the item or topic down, be as specific as possible. An example in law would be the Supreme Court case of <u>Brown v. Board of Education</u>, which ended more than a half century of state sanctioned racial segregation in schools. Why was this case significant? In this example it is easy to determine because the case was decided in 1954, and we have been able to appreciate the consequences of that case over the last 50 plus years. Ending racial segregation is public schools, eventually led to desegregation of other public places, such as swimming pools, libraries, restrooms, cafeterias, and public parks. In other words, the case is significant because it started a whole trend of related public desegregation. You may decide to choose a more recent topic or event, which may have not had consequences yet, but it likely to have implications for the future. For example, the discovery of more than

200 exoplanets outside our solar system. What might be the implications of these discoveries?

4. Prepare to explain to your group why you believe the item/topic is significant in terms they may be able to appreciate in their own lives. That is, how might this item/topic affect them personally?
5. Take turns presenting your item/topic to other members of your group
6. Group members will listen, but <u>cannot</u> ask questions during the explanation.
7. Group members will then give feedback to the presenter as to whether they did or did not appreciate the significance of the item/topic. What was or was not helpful in transmitting the perceived significance of the item or topic?
8. Circulate until all members have presented

Group Reflection Questions:

As presenter, how did you feel or think about your efforts to portray the significance of your item? Was it easier or harder than expected?

As listener, how well did you appreciate the significance of the subject? How did you feel about not being able to ask questions?

Did any new ideas or alternatives come to mind as you gave your presentation? What might you change, if anything, the next time your discuss this topic? If you would not change anything, why or why not?

Appendix 5:

NOTICE and REQUEST for DeNovo Review
Law Courses

Date of Notice:_____

Class and Section:_____ Group Number _____

Date of Case Presentation: _____

Signature of Group Members (certifies that majority vote to appeal has occurred):

_____
_____
_____
_____

Basis of Appeal (Why Group Believes Group Score is not accurate)

_____
_____
_____
_____
_____

Group's Self Assessment of Group Presentation, based upon original Standards
For presentation:

Self Score: NOTE: Only select the standard which your group feels is not accurate.
PLEASE MAKE SURE TO ATTACH a Copy of the _Original_ Presentation Slides !

Clarity ___ Explain:

Depth ___ Explain:

Breadth ____ Explain:

Significance ____ Explain:

Relevance _____ Explain:

Accuracy _____ Explain:

Precision _____ Explain:

Logic _____ Explain:

Organization/Efficiency _____ Explain:

*The general interest standard can not be appealed because it is a request for subjective preference, which is not readily measurable.

FP rev 6-09

Appendix 6:

Centripetal Forces: Red Flags in Group Dynamics

There is a natural tension which exists when people work in groups. There are forces that tend to bring the group together in cooperation, and counteracting forces that are more responsive to individual egocentric needs or desires. These latter forces can become disruptive, and compromise a group's effectiveness. It is finding a balance between these opposing forces that is central to a successful group outcome. That being the case, it becomes incumbent upon the group participants to be vigilant regarding preliminary signs of what I call "centripetal" tendencies. Looking for subtle signs of behavior which may be suggestive of both the affective (emotional), and cognitive (thinking) precursors which can result in non productive patterns. The following guide is intended to assist each group in the early detection of detracting group behaviors, in order to resolve them in a timely manner.

To some extent, what I am asking groups to do may be somewhat at odds with western cultural bias toward autonomy and independence. Nonetheless, there are times in work or in life, where even these highly valued traits require some modification and compromise. Otherwise, we may find it difficult to get along with others, and get things done.

Red Flag Signs of impending trouble include, but may not be limited to, the following:

1. Avoidance and/or withdrawal behavior- doing ones "own thing" by being unresponsive to group challenges and demands.
2. Blocking behaviors- counterproductive or distractive behaviors during group meetings. This can be verbal or non verbal behaviors.
3. Defensiveness- when challenged regarding their level of contribution, an aggrieved party may feel they have too many other obligations and excuses which prevent them from pulling their share of the group work. This sort of "Obstacle-itis" interferes with group contributions.
4. Anger- feeling frustrated at not being able to go at their own pace, they may feel stifled by the group experience. This sometimes leads to the following.
5. Attacking behavior-verbal or non verbal behavior which is perceived to be hostile or derogatory by other group members.

One of the remedies for avoiding some of these problems is to continue to focus on the objective standards required for the group. That is, focus should be on whether each student's contribution is accurate, relevant, clear, logical, significant, etc.,

Although it may be difficult a times, continue to work through the resistance that these group activities sometimes create. Remember, only through resistance do we have an opportunity to become stronger. Most importantly, seek guidance and advice early on if these behaviors should begin to emerge. Good luck in your challenge.